THE
FLOATING
POWDER KEG

On the night horizon, over the lapping black waters of the Java Sea, an ominous light reached up toward the sky. Krakatoa, the most feared volcano in the Islands, was belching signs of deadly life.

But aboard the **Batavia Queen**, as it moved ever closer to the threatening eruption, other and equally dangerous pressures were building. The hatred between father and son. The lust between man and woman. The forces of greed and fear and treachery.

And at the helm, a silent, guilt-haunted man, embarked on a desperate gamble to expunge the shame of the past with an act of daring that many men would call mad...

Other Signet Books
by Michael Avallone

- [ ] **ASSASSINS DON'T DIE IN BED.** Ed Noon, former private detective, takes a role as "private spy" to the President of the United States and plays red herring to a killer. (#P3689—60¢)

- [ ] **THE FEBRUARY DOLL MURDERS.** Tackling a Communist spy ring with an ingenious plot to sabotage the U.N., private-eye Ed Noon, finds himself unwittingly transformed into an espionage agent upon whose shoulders depends the freedom of the entire world. (#P3152—60¢)

- [ ] **THE GIRL FROM U.N.C.L.E.: The Birds of a Feather Affair.** April Dancer, female counterpart of those "Men from U.N.C.L.E." in the ABC network program, rescues a fellow agent kidnapped by T.H.R.U.S.H. (#D3012—50¢)

- [ ] **THE GIRL FROM U.N.C.L.E. #2: The Blazing Affair.** The intrepid Girl from U.N.C.L.E. downs three machete-swinging Mau-Maus without even chipping her manicure. Escapes from a ghastly trap in a South African diamond mine looking sexier than ever. But that's April Dancer—cool, gorgeous, and delightfully deadly.
(#D3042—50¢)

- [ ] **MISSING.** The President-Elect is missing! And Ed Noon, now the former president's secret spy, is elected to find him, while a whole nation trembles in pandemonium over the success of his mission. By the prolific bestselling author of 75 thrillers and mysteries. (#T3741—75¢)

THE NEW AMERICAN LIBRARY, INC., P.O. Box 2310, Grand Central Station, New York, New York 10017

Please send me the SIGNET BOOKS I have checked above. I am enclosing $_____(check or money order —no currency or C.O.D.'s). Please include the list price plus 10¢ a copy to cover mailing costs. (New York City residents add 5% Sales Tax. Other New York State residents add 2% plus any local sales or use taxes).

Name_____

Address_____

City_____State_____Zip Code_____

Allow at least 3 weeks for delivery

KRAKATOA, EAST OF JAVA

BY
MICHAEL AVALLONE

BASED ON THE SCREENPLAY BY
CLIFFORD GOULD

A SIGNET BOOK
Published by The New American Library

For John Jakes

Copyright American Broadcasting Companies, Inc.,
MCMLXIX

All rights reserved

SIGNET TRADEMARK REG. U.S. PAT. OFF. AND FOREIGN COUNTRIES
REGISTERED TRADEMARK—MARCA REGISTRADA
HECHO EN CHICAGO, U.S.A.

*SIGNET BOOKS are published by
The New American Library, Inc.,
1301 Avenue of the Americas, New York, New York 10019*

FIRST PRINTING, MARCH, 1969

PRINTED IN THE UNITED STATES OF AMERICA

THROUGH BAMBOO, DARKLY

Krakatoa was awake.

He stirred fitfully, his pitted monster's face scowling with monolithic grandeur. His serrated peak, a crown of awesome crater, spewed ugly black-red smoke, curling like death flags, into the slate-gray Java sky. Krakatoa snorted warningly, the smoke billowing violently. He lifted himself, rumbling and coughing. A jarring, crashing, thunderous tremor shook his massive body. The earth beneath him trembled.

Krakatoa was scarred, dark, ominous. The deep malevolence of centuries of violence shone from his mighty configurations of stone, rock and earth.

The rocky rim of his crater belched once more. He stretched his shoulders. The contained thunder in his bosom, subterranean and sinister, caused his peak to shudder. The giant moved restlessly. Random boulders, mighty rocks, flaked off his broad slopes, bounding down to disturb the seas below. Now, a great mushroom of intensely yellow smoke drifted from the top of his ancient head. Within his historic body, Krakatoa gurgled, rumbled and belched.

He was fully awake now.

The earth moved.

When Krakatoa was awake, his island waited and watched for his every move. The telltale signs, the omens, the displays of his uneasiness and discomfort. He was so like a god. And gods must be listened to or the wrath of Judgment Day will fall. Inevitably and remorselessly.

Krakatoa's stone lava-rim quivered against the curtain of sky. Percolating pools of sizzling lava, wildly colored, burst into dazzling fire-fountains. High-temperature bubbles exploded. Steam and heat unified in a spouting geyser of destruction. The boiling lava rose to the crater's rim, sloshing over the rocky lips, surging down into the valley below.

Krakatoa's island, named for him, saw the signs of his unrest. His displeasure. It was always the same when the sleeping giant tossed in his bed of rock and thunder.

All about the island, the tropical pools at the feet of mighty Krakatoa underwent a startling change. Blue-green water, so tranquil and lovely, bubbled and churned. The dark shade of ocher crept into the color scheme. And dead fish rolled to the surface, belly-up. Dead and sacrificial to Krakatoa's will.

Palm trees swayed, the tall bamboo leaned forward, birds cawed madly in flight. There was a burning stench of death in the vagrant Java winds. The earth shook and trembled.

Natives driving their sluggish oxen on the patches of stony farmland far below on the expanse of green island, paused to turn and look toward mighty Krakatoa. He was speaking and he must be heard. The mountainside was calling down to the valleys and the hills and the draws and the paddies. The natives, terror in their browned, hurt faces, huddled in the protection of gnarled trees. There was nothing man could do but wait. Until Krakatoa's displeasure was abated and he went back to sleep again.

But Krakatoa was in a restless mood this day.

A gigantic furrow appeared along the far side of the gnarled trees. The natives jabbered in fear. The earth split with a rending sound, the sudden fault in the fallow ground widening, lengthening, traveling swiftly. The ancient trees were wrenched from their mooring of roots and soil. The crunching groan of torn wood and ripped earth was a banshee wail of agony. The wind carried the sound, distorting it, magnifying every decibel of terror. Mighty Krakatoa had reached down and laid his hand on the land.

And the earth, the people and even the sea itself had been touched by his anger.

The quiet, sloping bottom of the Java Sea, with its floor of coral, sand and seaweed, undulated in the shadowy depths at Krakatoa's feet. A tremendous fissure, marked by a rising jet of bubbles, appeared on the sea's floor. The crevice widened and, with the widening, more gas escaped until, finally, a solid, muffled blast of explosion burst from the very floor itself, geysering water up through the murky green depths where it cannoned skyward. The sea churned and shook. White foam skyrocketed. Witless fish and inanimate sea coral and seaweed rained down.

Krakatoa grunted, almost smiling.

The yellow clouds of smoke funneling from his head blotted out the afternoon sky. The island waited, trembling in its fields, sampans and sandals.

Native women, their nets still spread across their sampans to dry, stared mutely at the angry volcano. The shrill shriek of the mountainous geyser of water rocking the sea could still be heard.

And then Krakatoa suddenly was supremely still. Hushed.

And the island took a deep breath.

And the school bell could be heard, tinkling softly on the newly quiet air. The whitewashed group of board buildings that were nestled on the rocky slopes of Krakatoa's kingdom were suddenly filled with the sound of children's voices raised in song. The two little island boys who had busied themselves with homemade telescopes, fashioned from bamboo shoots, to watch the mighty movements of old Krakatoa, hastened to rejoin their class. The order of nuns of the Jesuit cloth grimly and courageously resumed the tutelage of native minds. They crossed themselves whenever Krakatoa rumbled. Out of fear or the will of God, it mattered not.

Krakatoa had spoken.

Yet within the fragile building that passed for a schoolroom, the one of straw and white board, thirty children merged their voices in song. A patrolling nun, her cowl enormous in contrast to the little flock she shepherded, removed the bamboo shoots from the grimy hands of the two boys and motioned to them to pay attention to Sister leading the song.

The brave, plaintive Javanese melody, which no one could rightfully claim authorship of, seemed to hang within the thin white walls of the schoolhouse.

> *Sister, Sister, have you heard?*
> *I know a word that's a magic word:*
> *Just make a wish and say Kee kana lu,*
> *Kee kana lu and the wish will come true.*
> *Kee kana lu-oo.*
> *Kee kana lu.*
>
> *Sister, Sister, have you heard?*
> *If I should wish I could be a bird,*
> *If I should wish I could fly through the blue,*
> *If I should wish and say Kee kana lu.*
>
> *Kee kana lu-oo   Kee kana lu,*
> *Kee kana lu-oo   Kee kana lu,*
> *Kee kana lu-oo   Kee kana lu,*
> *Kee kana lu-oo   Kee kana lu.*

Sister, Sister, have no fear:
Kee kana lu makes the storm disappear.
There's nothing bad that will happen to you:
Just make a wish and say Kee kana lu.

Kee kana lu-oo   Kee kana lu,
Kee kana lu-oo   Kee kana lu,
Kee kana lu-oo   Kee kana lu,
Kee kana lu-oo   Kee kana lu.

The song hung poised on the air. Almost querulous, yet prayerful. The children's faces wore a massed smile, matched by the nodding approval of Sister.

Krakatoa had heard the song, too.

Wrathfully, scornfully, he flung down his cynicism, his disfavor.

A sharp rumble shook the frame building. Objects in the room tilted, clattered to the earthen floor. Fearful, the children exchanged looks. The sister leading the singing clapped her hands once more, signaling another chorus of "Kee Kana Lu." Her smooth face was a mask.

The children bravely took up the song again, voices rising slowly. The other sister went to the window and stared through the open area. Up toward mighty Krakatoa. He snorted again, fuming. The great ball of smoke hung in the sky.

The sister at the window crossed herself, with her back to the singing children. Krakatoa loomed awesomely on the horizon, bellowing and billowing.

Smoke poured from his crater.

The Java Sea washed restlessly against the shores of his island. Krakatoa, lying eternally just off the tip of the island of Java, was a volcanic master of all he surveyed.

In 1883 he was that of which legends are made.

BOOK ONE

THE BATAVIA QUEEN

Peaceful smoke drifted from the single squat stack of the *Batavia Queen*. The steam whistle shrilled, scattering a covey of white gulls searching the dockside for scraps of refuse. The hot, torpid clutch of the heat wave which had closed over Singapore carrying in its wake seven days of torrential rain had left the new morning in monumentally foul shape. Perspiration and mildew clung to every square inch of the *Queen*. For a knockabout tramp steamer converted from sail to steam but rigged for the former just the same, the *Queen* had endured much in her time. The signs of age and early erosion showed in her paint-flaked, black steel hull. Her decks, boasting the twin masts fore and aft, seemed ancient in the dull haze of daylight. Every flaw, crack and fault lay exposed as the hull of the *Queen* nestled alongside the dock. Her second deck, bustling with busy seamen readying the ship for the open seas, throbbed with the sounds of activity. On the boat deck below, the initial tasks were being instituted; the ones that precede any voyage. Yet this day was to prove a mixed bag indeed. Never had the *Queen*, with thousands of sea miles logged, ever carried such a diverse load of passengers.

The sticky heat, the screaming gulls, the blasting whistle and the salty stench of dockside intermingled with the smell of fish, fuel and sweaty seamen. All of those things Captain Chris Hanson had pushed to the back of his mind. He stood at the head of the gangplank, supervising the sailing, as was his custom. Yet even as he smiled bleakly in the dull blaze of morning, he was keenly aware of the new role he had assigned to his ship.

He was a tall, imposing-looking man in the single vertical brass-buttoned blue uniform of ship's captain. The stiff round collar of the tunic mounted an impressive face, finely boned, dark-haired and highlighted with piercingly keen eyes. Hanson wore a trim beard, sparsely bordered along the bronzed jaws, only to fan out in the approved Van Dyke spade tip at the chin. The Dutch East Indies, despite its motley melting pot of races, creeds and customs, had found most of the younger men in their thirties of a mind on one point of personal habit. The trim Van Dyke was most attractive on men. The ladies seemed to endorse the foible, too. Hanson was no ladies' man; the *Queen* was his woman, inevitably. As centuries of ship's captains before him, Hanson thought of his ship as "she." The supreme accolade. The mark of the yielding of one's love, admiration and affection to a great lady.

A dockyard donkey engine, chugging into view dockside, blasted Hanson's reverie with an ear-shattering scream of its whistle. He tugged the bill of his officer's cap farther down on his brow and scowled at the locomotive pulling alongside. A crowd of interested, awed natives, children and older people, had flocked about the flatcar attached beyond the engine. Hanson sighed. Even for Singapore, Mr. Douglas Rigby's diving bell was something out of the ordinary. Hanson viewed its slab-sided bright red contours with a mixture of disbelief and grudging admiration. Whatever claims the young English scientist made for his contraption, it was certainly outstanding to the eye. Members of Hanson's crew herded the crowd away from the flatcar, securing ropes and pulleys, yelling Dutch taunts to the natives. Hanson brushed his hands together and looked to the gangplank curving limply into the dirty Singapore bay.

Yes, he had taken upon himself and the *Queen* a mixed bag indeed. He had a fleeting moment of alarm but shook it off. Sailing always brought minutes and seconds of tension; when one is about to embark on a long voyage, it is as if one were leaving the earth and the society of mankind behind. The great unknown lay beyond every trip across the limitless seas.

Still—

There was no more time for idle, schoolboy reflections. He had spotted the large steamer trunks piled to the right of the foot of the gangplank. There, also for the world of Singapore to see, was gaudy paint, the trappings of show people. And as remarkable as Rigby's weird diving bell lay a mammoth ascension balloon, its globular enormity loudly proclaiming the presence of another legend: THE FLYING BORGHESES. The father and son who earned their precarious living as sideshow freaks of a sort. "Aeronauts" was the curious term.

Beside the balloon's wicker gondola stood two men. Obviously the Borgheses themselves. Hanson had little trouble spotting the Italianate stamp of them. The older man, taller, elegant, was as courtly as any nobleman, the beaver hat and expensive cut of his clothes lying on him impeccably. There was a grandiose worldliness to the man; rather than flamboyant, it simply indicated to the observer that here was the master showman. The Barnum species set down in Romany mold. As for the younger man, Hanson detected a sullenness and a discourteous disrespect in a face that could be no more than twenty years of age. The son also seemed restless, inattentive to his father, as the latter with gestures and low-voiced comments waited for the safe transport of the priceless balloon up the gangplank. Hanson studied the Borgheses, sensing he was watching some continual warfare that had never really known a proper ending. Only a fitful truce. It was all too apparent in the weary resignation of Borghese the Elder and the truculent moodiness of Borghese the Younger.

Deck noises grew, a winch cable squealed and the donkey engine grunted. Smoke rose over the dock. Behind Hanson, the voices of the crew, a medley of complaint, good-natured cursing and small talk, unified in a symphony that always accompanied sailing days. Hanson took some measure of comfort from the sound. The men would be busy, hoisting Mr. Rigby's diving bell on board, seeing to the Borghese balloon. It was well that there were chores and tasks to be done. It kept Hanson's mind off the rather precarious aspects of the strange voyage he had set for the *Batavia Queen*.

The Borgheses were moving up the gangplank now. Hanson waited for them, fixing a blank smile on his face. He had not misunderstood the family scene below. The older man was laying a restraining hand on his son's arm as the boy tried to push up the gangway ahead of him.

"Sons must show a certain respect for fathers, my boy. Whether they feel it or not."

The comment, as low as it was, reached Hanson. The young man hung back, a flash of dark anger on his youthful face. Hanson turned away, a pretext being presented by the appearance of his first mate at his side. Jacobs, who would never look clean-shaven because of his dark, pocked face, murmured something.

The elder Borghese, drawing his son behind him, smiled at Jacobs effusively.

"Captain Hanson—Giovanni Borghese . . ."

Jacobs nodded. "Signor Borghese . . ."

"May I present my son . . ." Borghese compounded the mistake. He gestured proudly to the boy at his elbow. "Leoncavallo."

Jacobs coughed. "I think you should know—"

Giovanni Borghese ignored him, pausing to garland Jacobs with a compliment. "Is he not every inch a captain, my son?"

Jacobs cut in swiftly, jerking a thumb at Hanson. His slitted eyes were not amused. *"This* is Captain Hanson."

Borghese's handsome face broke apologetically.

"Forgive me." Yet even as he spoke the words, his scrutiny had measured the quiet command of Hanson. The sun-darkened features, the trim beard, the electrically masculine black eyes.

"Buon giorno," Hanson said.

Borghese mildly addressed his son.

"This is a beautiful ship, is it not, Leoncavallo?"

The boy stared back at him steadily. For the first time he spoke, and Hanson could hear the deadly rivalry in his voice.

"Rome is beautiful."

With that, he wheeled and stalked down the deck. Slightly embarrassed, Borghese looked at Hanson. Hanson's face was expressionless. Jacobs shifted on his feet uneasily. Borghese managed a slight bow, then he, too, turned and followed his son.

Jacobs eyed Hanson and grunted under his breath before moving off.

Captain Chris Hanson thumbed his beard speculatively. Not even under way, and there was trouble in Paradise already.

Again, there was little time for second thoughts. The large wicker basket of the balloon was being hauled on board. Hanson stood to one side as the Chinese-Malay laborers toted the contrivance past him. The ever-reliable coolie labor, attainable for a bowl of rice or a bottle of gin, easily bore the basket over their heads. Hanson directed them to the hold, barking orders in fluent Cantonese. When he turned back to the gangplank, he was surprised to see the boarding ladder mounted by an attractive, slim Japanese girl. She wore the island costume of sarong tightly wound about her shapely figure. Her black hair, plaited back in a bun behind her head, glistened in the daylight. She was a lovely young thing. Hanson looked her over appreciatively.

"Captain Hanson?" Her voice was musical, lush. "I am the diver Toshi."

Hanson nodded. Of course. He had been expecting divers. "Where are the others?"

"They're here. We would like your permission to bless your ship and all those on her."

"I should be honored."

Hanson knew no God but the sea, no laws but those of ships, no Devil but he who fouled up a propellor screw. Still, he had learned never to take anyone's religion from them. Never to question or harass the ways and wants of superstitions. To keep a crew and a vessel happy, to maintain the spirits of the passengers, he would bow his head, cross himself and allow the invocations of God and Good Luck. There was just no other way.

The lovely young diver, Toshi, had turned and gestured with a hand that resembled a graceful bird. Up the boarding ladder filed three more youthful Japanese girls. Living replicas of Toshi's beauty and size and serenity.

As the girls came forward, their light, pleasant voices blended in song. Hanson paused to listen. Toshi led them toward the fo'c'sle, her own lips mouthing the words.

> *Blessed are the gods of water*
> *And blessed be the men who*
> *Go down to the sea in ships.*
> *Blessed be this ship and all aboard her;*
> *Blessed be the captain who*
> *Guides her over the waters.*

It was more chant than song, prayer than melody, but the harmony of the voices and the visual attractiveness of the singers had created quite a stir midships. Hanson's crew, burly, sweaty, tired, had stopped in the very middle of their diverse labors and duties to ogle and stare in open-faced admiration. Toshi and her three partners had descended belowdecks. The chant had halted but it lingered on the fine salt air. Hanson's eyes frosted over and he clapped his hands sharply. God was one thing, running a ship properly was another.

"Thank you," he called after the girls. To his men, he roared his will, "All right! Back to work!"

Sheepish and grinning, the men returned to their tasks. Up forward, Jacobs was marshaling the women to their quarters. Hanson strode to the inboard ladder to oversee the activity on the dock below. It was time for Mr. Douglas Rigby's invention to be taken care of. Hoisting it aboard the *Queen* would not be easy.

The diving bell, slab-sided and brightly crimson, was being

rigged with ropes and hawsers for transfer to the ship. From the native warehouses, veritable swarms of poorly clad coolies had come to watch the operation. Their jabbering and excited gestures filled the air. Hanson stared coldly down at the bell. The name *Butterfly III* shone ludicrous and absurd, painted in yellow letters on the sides of the weird device. Added to that was the sight of Mr. Douglas Rigby himself. He was moving about the bell, pointing and directing the laborers with great enthusiasm. Hanson restrained a snort of disgust. Rigby was a prototype of his class. Young, thatch-haired, beardless, an eternal boy. Wearing the off-white tropical suit affected by so many of the Englishmen one saw in the ports of Europe and Asia. The old school tie and do-or-die for dear Oxford. Hanson frowned. He could appreciate enthusiasm, even condone experimentation of a scientific nature, but there was too much of the boy playing with an expensive toy in the young man's makeup. A toy that could cost the young fool his neck if he was wrong in his watery calculations.

Hanson took the gangplank down, noting that the sun was already portside. A good wind, favoring the sailing, had picked up behind the *Queen*'s stern. Hanson seldom used sail anymore, thanks to the steam fittings of the ship, but a corner of his captain's soul still hankered for the open sea with full sail and a stout wind at his back.

Young Rigby spotted him and immediately flagged him down with enthusiasm. The young scientist's face was awash with pleasure and expectation. Hanson joined him at the flatcar where the great red diving bell stood like something on exhibit in a museum.

"There she is, Captain," Rigby bubbled over, his accents of British manhood stamping him for a lifetime. "Quite a veritable gem. You will be careful with the loading?"

Hanson's eyes roved over the red bell. He shook his head admiringly.

"We'll take care of it. You built that yourself?"

Rigby looked solemn. "With the frightfully expensive help of fifty native boys."

"Beautiful monstrosity," Hanson murmured. "Butterfly Three. Think it will work?"

"I think I've corrected what sunk the first two." Rigby fell into a painfully serious sigh. "All that money sunk into my marine experiments. I was rich once, damnably rich." He broke off, looking at Hanson with a plea in his eyes. *"You think it will work?"*

"You're a great scientist, Rigby. You'll get your money back."

"My *father's* money," Rigby blurted bitterly. "If he knew what I've done out here . . . if he were alive today, he'd turn over in his grave." Rigby changed the subject, avoiding an obvious Waterloo in his past. "You said there would be other scientists on board?"

"That's right."

Rigby had suddenly caught sight of Toshi and her three native companions on the forward deck. The Japanese girls were in a sprightly mood, fluttering their graceful hands, engaged in low, spirited conversation. Their voices rose flutelike on the wind.

"Who are they?" Rigby asked, turning back to Hanson.

"Scientists, Mr. Rigby," Hanson said with great care. "Marine scientists."

Douglas Rigby blinked. Hanson chuckled. But the chuckle went silent as an ominous, thumping drumbeat echoed from the shore. The beat was a monotone, the muffled cadence of a march. Hanson frowned and compressed his lips in a grim line. He had never liked the sound of a drum when he had come to know how it imprisoned men, made animals of human beings and took away all earthly dignity and honor. Now he saw what he did not want to see. The dock was filling up. A long, weary, shameful line of more than two dozen men were trooping into view. The gawking crowds were falling back, jabbering anew. Shouts and curses filled the air, only to drop away and dissolve in the deep steady beat of the drum. Two foot soldiers, uniformed and armed, were guarding the procession of convicts. At the fore of the line, a mounted officer pranced like some idiotically pompous general at the head of an advancing army. Hanson turned away, growling at Rigby: "Why don't you get your gem rigged for loading?"

Rigby nodded and swallowed nervously, recognizing a mood he didn't understand but had best be wary of. He moved off, and Hanson waited patiently for the details of this sudden surprising visit of men in leg chains, men treated as animals. The stained, perspiring bodies looked pitiful and wasted in the sunlight.

Hanson, stony-faced, mounted the inboard ladder to get a better look at the convicts. The unshaven, bearded, grimy faces were a sea of strangeness. The prancing officer on horseback was now shouting instructions to the uniformed guards. The convicts waited, a solid phalanx of whipped, defeated mankind. The harbor master, a fattish, heavily shouldered man named David Henley, was approaching from his shack office to the rear of the dock. He was still some distance from the gangplank when Hanson called down to him.

"Aren't those people on the wrong dock?"

The harbor master shook his head. "Afraid not, Chris." He hesitated, trying to smile and thinking better of it. "They're your passengers. Thirty of 'em. Bound for Madura."

Hanson stared down at him.

"I'm not going near Madura," he said flatly.

"No other ship seems to be going as close as you." Henley's tone was wheedling though edged with authority.

"Get those convicts away from the ship." Hanson bit out the words, each a dart of objection and disgust.

Henley winced at the sound. "I've been authorized to offer you two pounds per man." He put a soiled shoe on the gangplank.

"I'm not equipped to carry convicts." The clipped speech, a pounding hammer on the anvil of each word, exploded on the air. The harbor master still tried. He had a job to do, too.

"Or if you seem stubborn, to go as high as four. Which do you prefer? Two? Four?"

"Get the hell out of here!"

Henley took on some iron. "Four pounds a man, Chris. How's that?"

"It's no good!" Hanson shouted, trying not to ball his hands into fists.

Henley was holding up a packet, persistent in the face of the famous Hanson balkiness. His fleshy nose was mottled in the sun.

"If you'll just sign here . . ."

"I'm responsible for my crew and passengers," Hanson said with deadly calm, his voice a hiss.

"They won't be in the way," Henley said equably. Hanson came down the gangplank, drawing abreast of him. He confronted the harbor master.

"I've no room! Where do you expect me to put them?"

"In the hold."

"In the tropics?" Hanson was furious at the thought. "They'll be climbing the bulkheads."

Henley flung a look at the waiting line of convicts.

"They can't climb far in chains, the poor devils."

"They can't *eat* chains, either—I've no food for them."

Henley had been harbor master for too many seasons to let minor obstacles prevent him from obeying the rules and orders of his superiors.

"Their rations are on the dock. Chris—there's no choice,

actually. It's government business. Of course, if you decide not to sail . . . or unless you'd like your ship impounded." Henley managed the smile of the weaker man who wins over the stronger only because he is holding high cards. Hanson glared at him for a fixed moment and then he reached for the packet of papers and signed his name with Henley's pen. Without looking over his shoulder, he flung the packet airily to Jacobs, who had descended the gangplank behind him, waiting for more instructions. Henley nodded to one of the armed guards at the head of the chained wall of human flesh. The guard was brutal in appearance. A battered-nosed, deeply scarred face atop a body as wide as a wedge. He stationed himself at one side of the plank. The drum sounded again. A leathery hollow thump of doom. In measured but dragging tread to its beat, the long line of convicts began to shuffle up the gangplank. Hanson flung a scornful look at the officer on the horse, making a parade-ground affair out of something that at best was base and bestial. Henley wiped the sheaf of English money in his thick fingers and began to count off the agreed-upon amount. Hanson turned his back on him and strode away, leaving the details of the matter to the faithful Jacobs. He did not look at the long line of convicts. He stared straight ahead, unseeing. The drum thump-thumped its hollow message of despair.

With all that was on his mind and his plans for the voyage, the sudden addition of a hold full of desperate men—perhaps thieves, cutthroats and murderers—well, that was taking on cargo that could only mean trouble.

The balloonists, the Borgheses, had their questionable uses. A risk. The diving bell and Rigby would also serve an end. A justifiable end. And the Japanese diving ladies could be put to the test, advantageously too. They might be able to discover things in the sea that aeronauts and diving bells could not. But the thirty convicts—of no use whatsoever. Only an additional hardship. Thirty hair shirts that would make his back extremely uncomfortable. And then, of course, there was Harry Connerly, the diver, and his deep-sea reputation that was a marvel. And, inevitably, Laura. Laura Travis. The woman and the reason for all of the *Batavia Queen*'s preparations for the high seas.

Connerly.

Laura.

Hanson fumed in sudden irritation.

Where the devil were they?

From long habit he checked the ball of sun where it glowed like an enormous orange in the tropical sky. It had moved a full five degrees westward, raining down a golden, mist-laden atmosphere of prickly heat waves and hazy light rays. Hanson squinted at the dock, watching the last of the bedraggled convicts disappear onto the decks of his ship. Well, that part of the dirty business was done. He felt ashamed for his vessel and crew; to have to take part in the dirty business of the Singapore Government. To carry wretched human cargo bound for the torments and horrors of the prison camp at Madura. He had heard enough of Madura to position it alongside Devil's Island as a port of lost hope for human beings. The veritable end of a man's world. Where all decency, humanity and tenderness had fled.

When the drum had ended its forlorn rhythm and the guards and the horse officer had vanished among the teeming natives of the dock, Hanson once more boarded the *Batavia Queen*. Jacobs was waiting for him, holding out a thick sheaf of English pound notes. Hanson took the offered money without comment and went to the railing to count. He didn't trust Henley. Harbor masters were notoriously bad mathematicians. Rigby's diving bell was being secured with thick cables now, dockside. It would only be moments before the whole tricky business of storing the contraption in the hold would begin.

Lost in contemplation of the amount of money in his fingers for the transporting of human cargo, he was unaware of the arrival of a four-wheeled carriage on the dock below. Nor did he see the man and woman alight. The man turned to wrest belongings from the floor of the vehicle while the woman, as gay as any brightly feathered bird in the sunlight, traipsed up the gangplank of the *Batavia Queen*. Hanson might have been amused by the spectacle. The woman carried a needlepoint carry bag in one hand and a clay flowerpot with a long-stalked, sad-looking flower in the other. The hands belonged to a tall, sunny-faced, vivacious young blonde whose attractively longs legs moved her with eternal optimism. She was amply endowed with shapely hips, high erect bosom and a winning smile. More than one busy seaman on the decks of the *Queen* turned to look with admiration.

The woman paused halfway up the gangplank and brightly called out to Hanson, "Well, well well. . . ."

Hanson, turning, looked up. For a moment he showed his surprise and his pleasure. The woman on the gangplank exuded the sensuality of some of the native women one saw in the bars and on the docks, or in the beaded-curtain alcoves of back-street boudoirs. Yet this clearly was an American woman. No one else would emanate so much open-faced, touristlike curiosity. The woman was one of those blessed females that seem completely unaware of their natural, honest femininity. Hanson liked the woman at first sight.

She eyed him with candor. Not even the flowing skirt and prim cut of her gossamer-sleeved bodice could make her seem dainty.

"Why the 'Batavia Queen'? I mean, why 'Batavia'?"

He could see that the painted name of the vessel had captured her interest. She was staring at it along the hull.

"That was originally her home port," Hanson said softly.

The woman tilted her head inquiringly, puzzled.

Hanson smiled. "Batavia . . . Java."

Understanding dawned on the sunny face. The woman reacted wholeheartedly. Continuing up the plank, she swept aboard the ship, her encumbered hands waving. The longstalked flower drooped some more.

"That's nice," she exclaimed. "I never thought of it like that. A ship having a home or anything. Are you Mr. Hanson?"

"I'm Hanson."

With a rustle of silk she was upon him, thrusting the tall plant into his arms. From the needlepoint carry bag, she quickly produced a small pasteboard card, poking it at Hanson.

"Charley Adams," she announced herself gaily. "Social occasions, weddings, smokers."

Amused, Hanson eyed the card. "Soprano," he read aloud. Charley Adams laughed. Her tone was bright, vibrant, happy. Before he could comment further, he was aware of the man stepping around her. A battered white sea cap rode rakishly astride a head both broad and furrowed with lines and deeply burned skin. There was great physical power evident in shoulders bursting against an open-throated cotton pullover shirt. Squinting, deep blue eyes, twinkling yet dangerous, surveyed Hanson easily. The barrel chest tapered down to slim hips and trousered legs. Hanson stared back at the man who was obviously Charley Adams' traveling companion, or the reverse was true. When a man has known the depths of the deep blue sea as long as Harry Connerly had, he is bound to look exactly as Harry Connerly did. Spoiled, weather-beaten, lined. Yet with all that, virile, powerful and formidable.

A random shingle of red hair rode on Connerly's forehead. Patches of more red hair gleamed on his chest where it lay exposed beneath the cotton shirt.

"Hanson? I'm Harry Connerly."

"I know."

The man looked at him with that squint, yet it was no more than a searching politeness. For all his size, his voice was gentle and soft.

"We've met?"

"I know your work. That's why I hired you."

Charley Adams nodded approvingly. "He's the best underwater man there is."

Connerly ignored that. "You're salvaging a wreck?" Hanson nodded, too. "How deep is it?"

"According to the chart—if it's where we think it is—about eighteen fathoms."

Connerly frowned. "Six eights, that's forty-eight. Push out four, that's . . ."

Hanson took a moment to let him continue his calculations. "A hundred and eight feet," he said firmly.

Connerly's face showed no reaction, though Charley Adams had glanced at him quickly.

"We're working on straight shares?" Connerly asked soberly.

"It's a gamble," Hanson reminded him.

"What's the division?"

"Fifths."

"How about some money up front?"

Hanson shook his head. "We share and share alike."

Connerly looked doubtful. "I don't know . . ."

"Don't do it, Harry," the woman said instantly. "I mean if you have any doubts at all . . ."

Hanson shrugged. "Think about it."

"Harry, I don't think you should." Her voice had a fresh sound. Worry, now. Hanson smiled. He stared at Connerly.

"Just make up your mind before we sail. I wouldn't want to abduct you."

"Hanson . . ." Connerly set his mouth. He managed a tight grin. "Suppose I say no? You got another diver standing by?"

"I could always put on a suit myself. But you'd do the job better."

"But I can't even raise front money," Connerly protested. "Not even a hundred pounds?"

Hanson shrugged again, wagging his head. Connerly, his gimlet eyes fastened on the last of the convicts entering the hold of the ship, looked suddenly crafty.

"How many convicts are you carrying?"

"Thirty."

Connerly rubbed a finger around the tip of his nose. He smirked. "I happen to know the Dutch Government pays from two to four pounds a man." He grinned at Hanson. "I'd guess you got four. That's a hundred and twenty pounds. Gimme half, sixty pounds." He held out a weathered, muscular hand.

Hanson hesitated only a moment. The transaction was far more to his liking than the pitiful deal with Henley, the harbor master.

"All right." He laughed. "Courtesy of the Dutch Government." Connerly matched his grin and turned away. Charley Adams, the sunshine of her face touched by a cloud of something Hanson didn't understand as yet, followed him. But not before Hanson, bowing slightly from the waist, had returned to her the sad-looking plant. Connerly, sea bag and some extra gear bundled under one arm, led her off. Miss Adams' long legs flashed enticingly from a rear view. Hanson watched them go with a mixture of satisfaction and vague apprehension. The woman's attitude clearly hinted at something wrong. Damn the day and damn the morning. Something was not quite right about this sailing. He was unable, as was his usual style, to put his finger on exactly what. It was the damnable unlucky business of the convicts that had put him in such a bad mood. The *Batavia Queen* had never had the stench of the slave deck in her sails. Running human cargo smacked of the very same thing. A bad omen, all in all.

Creaking, straining cable sounds from the dock drew Hanson's attention once more. Rigby's infernal diving bell, secured by thick cables to the forward cargo boom, was being rigged at last for its hoist to the main deck hold. A Malay had clambered atop the bell with careless ease, one brown hand on the cable hook, a half-eaten mango in the other. Beyond the bell, Hanson spied a carriage approaching. A brisk two-wheeler rattled jerkily to a bouncing stop at the foot of the gangplank. Hanson stilled the rising beating of his heart. He maintained a calm he did not feel. The young woman stepping down from the fender of the carriage was unmistakable. She was receiving a single valise from her driver and now she turned to take in a full view of the loading of the *Batavia Queen*. Hanson hurried to the gangplank. The woman, calm and serenely beautiful in her tasteful frills and finery, had stooped to pick up an object from the dirty ground of the pier. Then she gathered her skirts about her and came up the gangplank where Hanson stood to greet her. Cargo-carrying stevedores and scurrying seamen bobbed about him, but Hanson was oblivious to everything but the face of Laura Travis. The quiet, impressively lovely face of the only woman he had ever cared about. He reached for her, smiling, his eyes telling her how glad he was to see her. With his hands anchored about her slim waist, he guided her down to the deck beside him. For a long rich moment, they looked at each other.

She broke the spell first.

"Are they here yet?" There was nervousness and anxiety in her voice. Hanson assented with his eyes. Relief flooded her smile. Her fingertips strayed to his shoulders affectionately.

"I didn't even say hello, did I?"

He said nothing, drinking his fill of her.

She opened a clenched hand, holding it out for his inspection. "Look what I found on the dock—a penny. That means good luck, doesn't it?"

A sweaty sailor hurried by, brushing into her. Hanson caught her about the waist, pulling her out of harm's way. His flesh trembled at touch of her. The sweet smell of her lingered in his nostrils. He held her close, seeing Rigby's awesome bell, swinging upward on its thick cable, the Malay seaman still poised like an acrobatic monkey on the cone of the steel sphere. Hanson's eyes went back to Laura Travis.

"You know about Krakatoa?" she whispered, searching his eyes. He nodded glumly, still gazing up at the bell riding high above the forward hold which loomed beneath it. A dark maw to receive a bright gift. All the deck activity had been suspended, everyone's attention focused on the new operation. Hanson held his breath, mindful of Laura Travis' closeness to his body.

The Malay was clinging with one hand to the big hook connecting the cables to the bell. He called out to a seaman below, gesturing with the half-eaten mango. He pretended to throw it, and the seaman ducked. The cables squealed and the bell hoisted over the deep black hold. Riding the capsule as though it were some incredible horse, the Malay hooted and jabbered his delight at the importance of being on top of the world. Hanson scowled angrily.

The guide rope strained, tautened. There was a protest of power and weakness. Abruptly, with no warning at all, a piercing snap of sound knifed through the atmosphere above decks. The diving bell began to spin dizzily in a wild, erratic orbit.

The bewildered Malay, suddenly riding a runaway horse that coruscated and whirled in mad circles, lost his grip on the cable hook. With a shriek of sheer terror and horror, his brown body was pulled from the revolving ball. He plummeted into the mouth of the dark hold where the scream was cut off with startling suddenness. The deck, the hatch, the dock and the sea closed off the scream for eternity.

Releasing Laura Travis' shuddering figure, Hanson sprinted for the hold ladder. The onlookers, frozen in a universal tableau of shock, fear and mortal bewilderment, could only stare. Yet, slowly, irresistibly, everyone, Laura Travis also, was drawn to the lip of the hatch to stare down at the tragedy below.

The winds of the seas suddenly scored over the decks of the *Batavia Queen*. The black smoke from the stack swirled and eddied on the heavy air. The feel and smell of death, as tangible to men who know the sea as the tang of salt water, clung to the sides and decks of the knockabout steamer.

Down in the suffocating confines of the hold, Hanson and a seaman knelt over the remains of the cable monkey. Crewmen and laborers hung back in an awed, silent semicircle as Hanson sought to wrest life from death. But to the onlookers above, the mute, clawlike posture of the lifeless figure smashed to the floor of the hold was testimony enough. Laura Travis covered her eyes, shuddering.

Hanson looked up from the corpse. The black seaman next to him, Squid, had been a close friend of the victim. Hanson touched his grimy shoulder, wordlessly. He climbed stiffly up the hold ladder, regaining the deck. No one looked at him or said a word. Laura Travis had seen the hurt expression on Hanson's face. She didn't wait to talk to him. She had moved off down the deck, gliding like a sleepwalker. She barely heard the whining, grinding sounds of the cables, guiding the arrested diving bell down into the hold where Squid had sorrowfully dragged the body of his friend to one side. Hanson walked to the rail, gazing mutely out over the waters of the harbor, the sun boiling hotly down into his eyes.

All his joy and gladness upon seeing Laura Travis again had gone up in smoke. In all the catalogues, lore and legends of the sea there is nothing on earth or under sky to match the preposterously bad luck that goes hand in hand with a death that occurs at sailing time. Not even the prospects of a fabulous voyage, an adventure that might make millionaires of himself and his crew, could alter the simple truth that the *Batavia Queen* had had a death on board.

Knowing the sea and the ways of seamen and ill omens, not even a hardheaded Dutch sea skipper like Chris Hanson could overlook the plain-faced calamity of the event.

The voyage was cursed now. Plain and simple. The mark of death was on the decks. The stench of the graveyard was in the boards. The ship was tainted with the blood of a

Malay seaman. It didn't matter that it was an accident, an unfortunate mishap. Those happened all the time. It was more that the seaman's death was an extension of the uneasy feeling Hanson had had ever since the thirty convicts had been foisted on him. He reflected ruefully on Laura Travis' finding of the penny. Good luck, she had said. Bad luck it had been. Rigby's blasted diving bell had already caused a death. A sticky, no-purpose death.

Squinting in the hazy light, Hanson pulled himself together.

Whatever the future or tomorrow's sea might hold in store for the expedition, it was time for the *Queen* to hoist anchor and quit the environs of Singapore harbor. A journey was in the offing. A journey into the realm of the treasure hunt, the search for El Dorado, King Solomon's Mines and perhaps the Holy Grail. Whichever lay at the end of the *Queen*'s search, Hanson was determined that the trip would be a success.

He had waited too long for Laura Travis to lose her now.

Jacobs materialized like a sour phantom at his elbow. The first mate had the second and third officers in tow. Hanson sighed. The chain of commands which would get the ship under way was almost automatic, and yet the procedure called for a practiced, overseeing eye. A ship's captain's eye. Jacobs and the second and third officers were all good men, but Hanson had never permitted any of them to put his ship to sea.

"Take in the plank!" Hanson barked curtly to Jacobs. To the third officer, he snapped, "Stand by the engines!" The officer ducked into the wheelhouse, giving the engine room telegraph a noisy crank. The ringing sound filled the bridge. Hanson cupped his hands, leaning over the starboard rail to shout to Jacobs who was now standing by on the fo'c'sle. "Let go all lines!" Toward the stern, he bellowed the order: "Let go all lines aft!"

The second officer, a Malay named Kuan, relayed Hanson's commands quickly. "Let go all lines aft!"

Seamen leaped to obey. The heavy hawser line, freed from the huge iron bitt on the dock, dropped gurgling into the water. The bow hawser followed, to be drawn aboard by the straining seamen. First Officer Jacobs supervised that important procedure. Hanson buried himself in the details of casting off. He hardly looked toward the rope locker where the thick dock line was being coiled by two powerful deckhands. Nor did he waste a glance on the small, sad procession of his crew transporting the dead body of the Malay seaman aft. Squid led the funeral cortege, his black face tear-stained and drained of life. Hanson did not want to see the effect of death on his men. He knew all too well its dangerous aftermath.

"Stand by at anchor," he shouted forward. "Ready!"

As Jacobs signaled the direction the anchor lay across the bow, with a wave of his arms, Hanson turned into the wheelhouse. "Slow astern!" he commanded the third officer. The engine room telegraph clanged in response. Hanson, his mind a blank, only concerned with clearing the harbor, raced carefully through the remainder of the necessary orders and instructions. Two short blasts of the steam whistle cord, blasts of two seconds each, followed the lifting of the anchor. Hanson called for a "hard port," "slow ahead," "midship the helm!" until finally the nose of the ship was pointed toward the wide-open limitless seas. A final glance at the operations of Jacobs, and Hanson gave the order that all the men were expecting and waiting for. "Prepare sail, Mr. Jacobs!"

The telegraph handle moved a notch forward, clanging again.

The *Batavia Queen* slowly, sturdily, pulled away from dockside. The body of the dead seaman lay silently on the rudder cable housing, covered by an oil-stained tarpaulin. Squid was lowering the red, white and blue Dutch flag to half-mast with slow, steady fingers. Hanson did not protest the action. Squid was a black giant from Trinidad, worth any two men on the ship. His sorrow would be a religion to him.

The paint-flaked, battered steel hull of the *Batavia Queen* plowed smoothly into the bay. In its churning wake, the scummy, ugly waters of the harbor washed against the dock pilings. The sea gulls cawed furiously, flapping for greater altitude, away from the trailing column of smoke belching from the solitary stack between the twin masts of the steamer. The jabbering natives and locals on the pier waved and poked their arms in gestures of admiration and contempt. The flaming sky, coppery and streaked with crimson smudges of soiled cloud-banks, was a mantle of haze and tropical discomfort across the far horizon.

Captain Chris Hanson bore down heavily on the steam whistle cord, shattering the stillness of the harbor. To drown out his sorrow, to crowd out his uneasy thoughts. His foreboding.

In a measure of comfort, he was happy, though.

For better or worse, come what may, the *Batavia Queen* was under way at last.

Laura Travis' benignly beautiful face was troubled. Sitting on the edge of the stout square bunk in her cabin, she presented a portrait of tragic contemplation. A white safari hat lay on the carefully tucked spread of blanket. Her trunk, valises and a pair of hat boxes remained where the stevedores serving as stewards had left them. She had not made a move toward unpacking since she had left Hanson topside. There was much of the madonna in Laura Travis' face. The wistful, hauntingly lovely quality of the *Mona Lisa*.

"Hello."

Hanson's clipped voice sounded from the doorway. She looked up slowly to see him standing in the passageway. He was smiling warmly, but she didn't miss the small black leather-bound Bible in his hands.

He stepped into the cabin proper, his eyes roving over the unattended luggage. His dark eyes twinkled.

"Would you like some help with your things?"

She shook her head, still staring forward, as if she were unaware of him. "Was the sailor . . . a close friend of yours?"

"He was a friend," Hanson said simply.

She stared dismally at the floor of the cabin. Her placid face was betrayed only by the emotion in her eyes.

"Truthfully, I feel very much like going back."

"There's nothing to go back to."

"No, I guess there isn't." She flashed him a sudden quick look. "The others, Chris. The people you hired. I don't *know* them . . . I'm frightened. . . ."

"You will know them," Hanson said promptly.

She tried to smile. It didn't come off. "I'd like to come to the dining room but not today. If it's all right with you. Could I have my meals here?"

"Certainly," he said sympathetically. Softly. "Today." He smiled again. "Tomorrow we will expect you."

He left the room, closing the door quietly behind him. She stirred herself from the bunk, reaching nervously toward the trunk and her valises. She darted the loneliest glance in the world at the closed door. She was a very frightened young woman now. Something she had never imagined herself to be. Certainly a thing she had not been when she had summoned enough courage to leave her life in Java.

A thumping, shuffling beat, falling in mournful cadence, came down through the wooden ceiling above her head. She started. The weird rhythm filled the narrow cabin. Her heart skipped fearfully. She waited, hands stayed in the act of unpacking a valise. Her eyes roved back and forth, following the insistent beat of the drum.

The fiercely pagan beat was supplemented by a low-pitched, human voice rising in a song for the dead. A native dirge.

She didn't know that the giant Trinidadian, Squid, was writhing in some timeless ritual death dance. Contorting, swaying, grieving, even as Captain Hanson, standing at the ship's stern with the other officers baring their heads, said a few last words from the tiny black Bible. The dead seaman, prone on a canvas stretcher at the starboard rail, was cast into the sea. The swathed, strapped corpse slipped silently, almost soundlessly, into the shifting waves. Squid concluded his traditional dance and moved slowly away, passing Giovanni Borghese. The tall black giant did not see the pain and tragedy in the Italian showman's eyes. There was no sign of the son, Leoncavallo.

The crew of the *Batavia Queen* lined the railing, each man alone with his own thoughts for a few seconds as Hanson closed the Bible, replaced his officer's cap on his brow and terminated the funeral. A hush had fallen over the deck, broken only by the wash of the winds, the rippling echoes of the sea in its endless monologue.

Tradition had been served. Burial at sea for a man who earned his livelihood from the sea. The wheel had spun full cycle. What the sea gave, the sea took back. In broadest daylight or blackest night.

As the men shuffled away from the rail, silent, moving like dead men, Hanson stalked to the bridge. He didn't say a word to Giovanni Borghese as he brushed past him.

A stiff breeze fanned across the decks of the vessel. Ratlines and furled sail made small, wrenching noises in the afternoon air. The sun dipped forlornly in the skies, trailing the *Batavia Queen* like some ardent suitor ever ready to plight his faith and promises.

Squid stood like a black statue atop the main hatch, closed over now with its lid of canvas-covered wood. The face of the giant was alien and immobile. He might have been cast in ebony.

Only his great hands, clenched in harsh fists, spoke of the agony and sorrow in his heart and mind.

Ship's bells tinkled from the bridge, sounding bright and Christmas-like on the soft, balmy air.

In the cabin where Charley Adams and Harry Connerly had set their bizarre luggage, Charley was hanging her dresses in the cabin closet, lamenting the small amount of space. Connerly, who had fished a battered newspaper from the mess of his diving gear, was stretched across his bunk, reading. Charley's clothes, all bright and feathery like the lady herself, lent dashing pastels and flamboyant oils to the neat yet drab cabin.

Connerly squinted across the top of the paper at her. Watching her bustle about like any housewife, which she certainly wasn't by any yardstick of social conduct, made Harry Connerly oddly uncomfortable. In his own private way, he had to fight off the feelings of guilt, of vague uneasiness it always instilled in him.

"Well, Charley," he grunted sourly. "You did it again. Givin' Hanson that lame-brain card o' yours. Weddings, smokers—*agggh!*" He shook his head, the red, shingle-like locks of his hair tumbling. For emphasis, he snapped the battered newspaper open to another double sheet.

"*And* social occasions," Charley added brightly, taking no offense whatsoever.

"Sure." Connerly hid behind the paper. "Social occasions. You used to put the piano player to sleep."

"Maybe. But I know how to keep *you* awake, Harry."

As always, she was unfazed by his lectures and kidding.

He snorted loudly. Charley Adams turned at that, discontinuing her closet operations. A sudden, mischievous smile dimpled her pretty face. Sauciness and perkiness flamed in her warm brown eyes. Connerly, buried behind his newspaper like a surly bear, was suddenly aware of a strange silence in the cabin. He lowered the paper and looked up. You could never tell what Charley Adams would do next. Never.

He might have known.

She was twirling slowly in a spiral of sensual abandon. She had changed to a sailor dress as soon as they had gone below and now her slender fingers were unbuttoning the top of the dress. The firm flesh of her bosom rippled, surging upward, released from the confines of one of her underthing contraptions. Connerly scowled, affecting a disinterest he didn't feel. Whatever a woman needed to ring Connerly's bell, Charley Adams had in spades. She was the only dame he had ever been able to stand for more than a night's fun. He knew it, and what was worse, she knew it, too.

She came toward him, undulating her hips, lowering the collar of the dress even farther. Coquettishly, her red lips and brown eyes were working now. Batting slowly with the eyes, moistening the lush mouth with a flicking pink tongue. Connerly growled. He tried to turn over, away from her. Now she was singing. The catchy, old-fashioned lament that was guaranteed to have them crying in their beer in any saloon along the Barbary Coast. Her voice wasn't bad, either. She had a husky voice that was *all woman*.

"*I'm looking for an old-fashioned boy* . . ."

She spun about him, orbiting in color and sexuality. The warm scent of her choked his salt-lined nostrils. At the close of her intimate little turn, she began to move out and away from him. But she had won her minor victory again. She won all the minor ones.

Connerly's big hand shot out, caught her by the waist and spun her violently into the depths of the bunk. He pressed his hard jaw into the softness of her neck. She didn't try to squirm away but subsided, folding her arms about him. Her warm body scalded him.

"Damn you," he said hoarsely. "*Damn you . . .*"

"Sure," she answered back, with a catch in her throat and that look in her eyes he had never been able to fathom. Not like he could a sea bottom where a wreck was supposed to lie. The look scared him. It was so damn . . . well . . . like *giving in*.

Even as he kissed her with almost brutal ferocity, his hands were pawing clumsily at her body. Searching, kneading.

Charley Adams closed her eyes and let him.

Her answer for everything that happened between her and Harry Connerly was *Love*.

His kind wasn't as good as hers but she was intelligent enough to recognize it as love all the same. Even if he didn't.

But it had always helped her to separate the men from the boys. And Harry Connerly was a *man*. The best kind of man. Strong and brave.

Neither Connerly nor Charley was mindful of the sudden pitch of the *Batavia Queen* to starboard.

First Officer Jacobs, with the necessary business of the funeral done with and now only a log entry, descended from the bridge, crossing the deck with his curiously shifting gait. He had been a seaman since his cabin-boy days along the China seas, and it had left him with that rolling, pitching walk that characterizes the lifetime sailor.

Jacobs found the burly uniformed guard on duty where the

prisoners' hold was accommodating the thirty chained convicts foisted on Hanson at the last second of sailing. The guard straightened when he saw Jacobs. His face was perspiring and tired in the fading sunlight, and his uniform had wilted.

"Captain wants to talk to one of your prisoners," Jacobs muttered. "Name's Danzig."

The guard whined nasally. "I can't do that. These are lifers. No deck privileges."

Jacobs stared the man down, bleakly.

"The *captain* gives privileges. Open up!"

The guard hesitated, then with an exasperated intake of breath, turned, calling into the black void behind him. *"Danzig!"*

Jacobs could hear the clicking, clanking shackles of the prisoners as they stirred and blinked toward the ladder where sunlight had entered their black hole of torment. Chains and manacles rattled in the hold. Jacobs waited until he was joined by a tall, lean, unshaven convict. There was a defiantly tight grin on the man's face. Jacobs didn't like his looks at all. He saw snakes and lizards and something serpentine and evil in the man called Danzig.

The guard had reluctantly loosened Danzig's chains from the links connecting him to his fellow convicts. Jacobs motioned Danzig across the deck, up to the bridge.

Hanson was alone on the bridge. Jacobs gave Danzig a friendly pat on the back and went below again. Danzig flicked his eyes in the light of the bridge. His dreary convict uniform, leg chains and generally unkempt condition were pitiful. The bright sky drew his attention and then the bright sea. Hanson watched him without saying anything, letting him adjust to his new freedom of movement and sight. Danzig turned back to Hanson, who put out his right hand. Danzig took it, shaking it with a preoccupied air.

"Well, well, Lester." Hanson surveyed Danzig from head to ankle chains. "I see you finally made it. What happened?"

"Killed a man in a fight."

Hanson lit a cigarette. "Who was he?"

"Never got his name, Cap." Danzig sounded rueful. Yet for all his weariness and weakness, the man's voice was a well-modulated rasp of tonal power. "Sou' sou'east . . ." He had keen inquisitive eyes, too. Hanson remembered that about him. "Madura?"

Hanson nodded, watching how Danzig had somehow navigated the ship even while in the dark hold.

"Eventually."

"Damn!" The expletive roared from Danzig's thin-lipped mouth. His lantern jaws worked. "Ah, that Dutch prison island's not so bad as it sounds. Madura. Fever buries the average con in less than three years. Fever and heat. Who's engine room chief now, Cap?"

"I moved Driscoll up to your spot."

Danzig nodded as if that were fine with him. Hanson studied him. "Anything I can do for you while you're aboard?"

Danzig thought a long moment. He feasted on the blue sky, the limitless sea. When his eyes came back to Hanson, there was a sudden fervor in the man not usually found in one who had been one of the coolest, most efficient members of Hanson's crew.

"Let me stay on deck, Cap . . . breathe air . . . eat by myself? It's a zoo down there." Danzig rattled his chains violently.

Hanson had made up his mind long before he had sent for the man. In fact, when he had spotted Danzig among the prisoners in the hold during a routine check with the burly guard, he had been surprised and then curious to learn what had happened to his former engine room chief. Now he knew, but the information hadn't altered his thinking. A man can kill for many reasons, not all of them of his own making. It was the way of the sea and the world and men. Hanson never chose to play the role of God, making judgments and punishments.

The entreaty in Danzig's eyes shone like a beacon.

"Please, Cap. . . ."

"You've got it."

Danzig licked his lips. The slitted eyes and the crafty face that had reminded Jacobs of snakes were suddenly cheerful.

"That's three days . . . isn't it, Cap? I better get busy, hadn't I? Mind if I go below for a look, say hello to Driscoll?"

"She's your ship," Hanson said quietly.

Danzig grinned his thanks, shuffling off. The chains sounded hollowly on the mahogany deck. Hanson watched him go, thoughtful and mildly puzzled. Then he stirred himself and craned his neck to see the condition of the rigging of the mast at aft. It had squealed like a sea rat all day and might want checking. He made a mental note to tell Jacobs. In a few moments he had forgotten all about Lester Danzig. Just as he had pushed to the corners of his mind the death of the Malay seaman, Laura Travis' sudden uncertainty in the face of death and the strange personalities of the aerialist Borgheses and of Douglas Rigby with his odd diving bell. For

Harry Connerly and his woman, he had few doubts. The love of the sea shone from the red face of the deep-sea diver. As for the four Japanese diving girls, they too were little to think of. It was truly unfortunate that Squid's friend had been smashed to death in a regrettable accident. Still, those things did and must happen, sooner or later. You cannot log thousands of nautical miles without some mischance.

At least, the *Batavia Queen* was having a smooth sailing. Twenty-seven miles out of Singapore and not a ripple of bad weather or yet a threat of the same.

There was a strong southeasterly wind and that was all to the good, too. It bid fair for a fine sailing.

Hanson puffed on his cigarette, his mind coming back to Laura Travis. His blood quickened. Laura Travis.

She seemed as lovely and as unforgettable as ever.

And perhaps, he mused ruefully, just as *untouchable*.

He hoped not.

It was night. Miles and miles of endless darkness yawned ahead. Brave stars twinkled in the heavens. The *Batavia Queen* rode gracefully on the calm and easy sea, etched lightly against the night sky. Her decks were quiet. There was an atmosphere of relaxation and languor aboard. No lights shone except the dimly lit oil lamps that were so necessary for seeing and reading the navigational instruments and charts in the wheelhouse. The wind keened softly in the rigging. A winch spindle groaned. A seaman yawned noisily. On deck, midships, a small group of the men stood in a huddled circle pegging their personal knives into a ring of coins. The men kept their voices low and their play down to a minimum of noise. Squid and other crewmen squatted silently between watches on the rudder cable housing at the stern. In the wheelhouse, the helmsman, Jan, stifled a heavy yawn that seemed to split his face in half. It had been a long and quiet night, broken only by an occasional murmur of voices and the sharp flight of knives zinging into the deck floor.

Suddenly, with no warning to signal the beginning of anything unusual or out of the ordinary, the distant horizon came alive. Far off to the portside of the *Batavia Queen*, the night sky lit up like a gigantic Roman candle. The night became day in the flash of an eye. The all-encompassing glare which seemed to illuminate one half of the world was now punctuated by a series of silent explosions of light—bursts of aerial brilliance as though some armada had abruptly touched off every single flare in their armories. But these were no mere flares. All the flares in the universe could not have equaled the brilliance or rocket-like explosions of light.

The crewmen leaped excitedly to their feet, pointing in awe at the first of the series of explosions in the southern sky. They flocked to the rail, jabbering like any collection of coolies on a dock. They were men who knew the sea, lived the sea and loved it, but there wasn't a man among them who had ever been witness to a phenomenon like this. It was unearthly and incredible. The sky was on fire, bathed in a great eerie crimson flood of illumination.

Douglas Rigby was eternally grateful, as any scientist would be, to have been on deck during the occurrence. Quickly, he extended a telescope, peered keenly and paused to jot important memorandums down in a small notebook. He was in a transport of excitement and intelligent curiosity. He too had never seen the likes of this. His smooth face glowed with the reflection of the glare. His thatch of yellow hair streamed in the wind sweeping along the deck.

Just below the wheelhouse, Hanson stood. He too was observing the apparition that had come out of the night like a sea monster. All too fantastic, all too weirdly beautiful and nautically inexplicable. Hanson had never seen such a marvel. He held his breath, amazed at the silent but fiery heavens. The great blaze of light burned brightly for long, almost unendurable moments of beauty and awe and wonder.

In the wheelhouse, Jan had been joined by Jacobs. Both men were rapt, their eyes riveted to the southern sky, the blazing pyre of light.

"What is it, Mr. Jacobs?"

"I don't know," Jacobs muttered, throwing a side glance at the compass, "but we're heading in that direction."

Jan swallowed, stunned into silence.

And then the illumination ceased. Shut down. Like the turning down of an oil lamp. Total darkness reigned in the skies. Jan and Jacobs squinted, straining to see the direction of the disappearance. The night was mockingly black again. Blacker and darker than before. There was no sign or evidence of the fiery display that had materialized like ghost riders in the sky.

"It's gone," Jan murmured in a faint, faraway voice.

Downstairs in the main salon of the *Batavia Queen*, the Borgheses, father and son, were engaged in a game of darts. The salon with its crystal chandeliers, finely grained wood, tasteful furniture and long mahogany bar seemed a proper setting for Giovanni Borghese. Hanson had spared no expense in furnishing the salon with the tribute and curios of a world of exotic ports and far-off places. Teak from India, oil canvases from Holland, silk lace curtains from the shops of China. All in all, an air of grand stateliness and royal splendor. It was quite a thing apart from the battered, knockabout aspect of the exterior of the vessel itself. Borghese found the salon an admirable place. Quite to his tastes and suitable to a gentleman of Italy. One saw rooms such as this in Milano and Firenze.

Yet the elder Borghese was annoyed. Leoncavallo, with that typical hostility of the son who had left respect for the parent with the toys he had abandoned as a child, was clearly in no mood to make peace. He was sullen and mulish, flinging his darts with undue ferocity into the board mounted tightly against the wooden length of one of the many pillars that supported the ceiling of the salon.

"We've never gotten along too well, you and I," Borghese said as he slammed one of his own darts into the circular face of the target. He followed it up with another throw. As accurate as the first, spearing the bull's-eye with true sportsman's skill. "And that is unfortunate because we only have each other."

Leoncavallo was lined up, ready to throw his share of the darts. His sullenly handsome face, crowned by a mop of unruly black hair, was defiant.

"That's not quite true. You have your women . . ." He paused to fire a dart. It thudded into the inner circle, close to his father's strike. "Your fine wines . . ." Another dart joined the first one. "And your tailor . . ." The last dart shot across the room, burying its needle point into the wood. "You don't need a son."

"I have needed a son very much," Borghese said wistfully. "And you have not been one."

Both men walked to the board, tugging the six darts from the wood. Their eyes met across the short space between them. For once, Leoncavallo did not look away, did not retreat into sulky childhood. He glared at his father.

"And I have needed a father. Perhaps we should place notices in the newspaper."

Borghese smiled wryly.

"I had hoped we might come away from the adventure with what family we have intact."

They returned to their places at the throw line. Leoncavallo began the next round.

"I just hope we come away from *this* adventure intact. And when we do and I have half your share, I'll soon be very far away from you." He flung his first dart.

"But not with that girl," Borghese interposed quietly.

"Don't command me, Father. You don't even know Francesca. You have only seen her a few times with me. . . ." He threw his second dart. His aim was bad. The feathered shaft spun off the board and clattered to the floor.

"I have seen her," Borghese said, "closer."

"I can make up my own mind," Leoncavallo blurted, now hurling his third dart in sheer anger. Borghese poised a dart, not looking at his son.

"Depend on your father." The dart thudded into the big circle. "You see, Leoncavallo, she is much older than you and—"

Leoncavallo wagged his head furiously.

"Papa, it's no good. You haven't given me one good argument. In all these weeks it still comes to people saying this or that about her. No proof. You'd do anything you could to stop me from seeing her."

"Yes," Borghese said firmly, throwing once more.

"Why?"

"She is . . . experienced. She is not for marrying."

Leoncavallo chuckled cockily. "And now comes either the story of Francesca and the old friend of the family or the—"

"He was not the only one," Borghese snapped harshly. He flung the last dart, walking forward to retrieve his set of three. His son gripped his arm at the elbow.

"He was a friend," Leoncavallo said, challenged.

"Not a friend. More."

The boy was not to be stopped now. His eyes had kindled with rage and jealousy and hurt.

"A *friend*," he insisted, still squeezing his father's arm. Borghese looked at his son. Defeat and sorrow mingled in his broad, smooth face.

"A man much older than she. A man old enough to be—"

Leoncavallo released him, not wanting to hear any more. He tried to run. The tilt of the deck floor seemed to stop him.

"Old enough," Borghese said unflinchingly, "to be *your father*."

The moment of shock was one that Giovanni Borghese was certain he would take with him to his grave. The revelation had crucified his son where he stood.

"That's enough!" Leoncavallo shouted, his dark face filling with crimson.

"Two years ago," Borghese went on, a litany of self-condemnation. "When you were still—"

"I won't listen! I don't want to hear any more!"

He tried to move away but he could not run fast enough from the awful words.

"There were others. I didn't flatter myself that Francesca—"

Leoncavallo's hand flew out, pinning his father to the wall next to the mahogany bar.

"That's enough," he rasped through clenched teeth.

Borghese did not struggle. He gazed helplessly into the face of the man he had reared from infancy. His classic head bowed. Leoncavallo's face, tears filling the eyes, shimmered before him. Still, it must be done. There was love in hurts, too.

"You are a son," Borghese said softly. "I know it must be every bit as difficult . . . as being a father."

Leoncavallo's right hand, balled into an angry fist to strike the face that was an image of his own, dropped weakly to his side. Sobbing, fighting to hold back the tears, the boy turned away from his father, and hurried from the salon.

Giovanni Borghese stared after him for a long moment. Then, with great slowness and grace, he moved to the bar where he reached for a cut-glass decanter and a tall matching glass.

His smile had all the sadness of generations of fatherhood in its contours.

Youth was such a wonderful, devilish time.

So hard on the young. The so very young. Like Leoncavallo.

But what of the vanity of all old fools who must imagine themselves still great shakes with the ladies? Like Giovanni Borghese.

Borghese sighed, pouring from the decanter.

There was nothing very happy about losing a son.

Not when he is all that you have left in this world.

Neither of the Borgheses, father or son, had been present on deck to witness the weird phenomenon of the bursting, brilliant lights on the far horizon.

The Flying Borgheses might have had a valuable opinion on the subject.

Douglas Rigby found the captain's quarters of the *Batavia Queen* very much to his liking. He had found admiration for the cut of Hanson's jib, but the *sanctum sanctorum* of the man was infinitely more rewarding. The quarters spoke volumes for the man, denoting quiet intelligence, the mind and attitudes of a scholar. Not to mention neatness and a sense of order in all things. Rigby was enough of a scientist to respect all these facets of Hanson's living quarters.

It was a double room, actually, half sleeping quarters with the remainder serving as office–chart-room–library. As Hanson paced in front of his desk, answering some of Rigby's pointed questions about the rest of the members of the expedition, the young scientist studied the room.

The desk, of fine dark wood of some exotic nature, held a large chart, annotated with red, black and green ink. Flanking the map were two brass oil lamps, ornately masculine. Beside the desk table was a large floor-model globe of the world in a rich wooden frame. Many books, expensively bound and obviously well-thumbed, were lined on shelves along the wall and lying on the desk. An armillary sphere and a battery of antique navigational equipment occupied another shelf. Rigby recognized sextants, mechanical and directional compasses and a Bausch & Lomb telescope. Some of the equipment was corroded, sea-rusted, resembling ancient salvage prizes. A heavy, carved pipe rack with numerous, carefully collected pipes was carelessly but conventionally located on another table. The walls, darkly wooden, held a school diploma and a framed photograph of the King of the Netherlands. A very battered and symbolic flag of Hanson's home country draped one wall of the sleeping compartment area. Brass oil lamps on the walls cast a quiet, restful aspect of the interior of the quarters. By the big bunk, a pile of reading material—books, magazines and periodicals—was stacked next to the lamp. Leather-bound chairs, like the one Rigby was settled in, filled the room. The spread on the bunk was a deep blue sailcloth. Or muslin. Rigby couldn't be sure. All in all, Hanson's fortress of solitude was a man's well-used, comfortable place.

Rigby's attention came back to Hanson. The captain had paused before his chair to aim a defensive forefinger at him. Rigby realized that some remark he had made had somewhat angered Hanson.

". . . you *both* work," Hanson growled. "With Borghese's height in his balloon he naturally has an advantage of seeing into the shallower waters over a wider area. You'll be in the deep water. You and your bell. What *he* can't see, you can. I'm using all the tools at my disposal, Mr. Rigby. That's why I've got two kinds of divers."

"Two kinds?"

"Yes. The four young Japanese girls are pearlers. They have mobility under the water. Connerly we will use for depth. I mean to find that wreck any way I can, as quickly as I can."

Rigby smiled apologetically.

"I wasn't complaining about your operation of the search, sir. It's really quite ingenious. It was just that the men were saying . . ." He stopped because Hanson overrode his sentence with impatience.

"You graduated from college, Mr. Rigby?"

"Oxford."

There was a knock on the door and Hanson called out sharply. "Come in." He returned his attention to Rigby. "A degree in science, I believe it said in your letter. Didn't they teach you anything about people there, Mr. Rigby?"

With his earnestness challenged and the interruption at the door on top of it, Rigby was confused. "Not . . . very much, sir," he admitted, baffled by the sight of Laura Travis, solemnly beautiful, standing on the threshold of Hanson's quarters. The woman was carrying a glass of water and a teaspoon of sorts. Rigby started to rise. Hanson waved him back down and beckoned Laura Travis forward. She found a chair and sat down quietly. Her deep-set eyes were unfathomable. Rigby had approved of her classic madonna-like loveliness since he had first set eyes on her topside. Breeding in every fine bone and line of her. No mistaking that. A thoroughbred.

Hanson rushed on, oblivious of the interruption, if it was one.

"People exaggerate. Forget the idle talk. The ship is full of it. I'm telling you now that it doesn't matter who finds the wreck—who brings up the safe—it is share and share alike on this ship. No bonuses, no competition. Is that clear? You, Borghese, Connerly, Toshi—you're equally important."

His heat flustered Rigby.

"Yes, sir."

"Goodnight, Mr. Rigby." Hanson's tone was cold now.

"I'm very sorry, sir."

"Don't be. Just come to me first next time."

Rigby seemed to bolt for the door, almost forgetting his English manners. He nodded hurriedly to Laura Travis and exited without looking back. Hanson sighed, looking at the woman.

"That sixty pounds to Connerly is coming back to haunt me."

"All part of being a ship's captain, Captain."

He raised his eyebrows at her sudden levity. She was smiling warmly. He watched her for a long moment, smiling too. She broke the spell, indicating the teaspoon and glass.

"I came to ask for something to help me sleep. I believe you have my medicine."

He crossed to a drawer of the desk, unlocking it. He rummaged in the drawer, faintly puzzled. "I think I put it somewhere in—" He produced a flat steel box, extracted several small envelopes from its interior and selected one. "Here it is." He held it up, reading the prescription aloud. "Half a teaspoon in a . . ." He frowned, broke off reading and looked at her. She stood before him holding out the teaspoon and glass.

He had not liked what he had read on the packet of powdered medicine.

"It helps keep me asleep," she said without apology. "This way I don't have to worry about the nights at least."

He measured out a prescribed dosage of the powder and dumped it in the glass. His eyes had not lost their beetled look.

She accepted the medicine from him, not taking her eyes off his bronzed face.

"Dear Chris," she murmured. "What's going to happen to us?"

He ignored the remark. "How long does it take for this to work?"

"An hour. Sometimes two." She was soft again, hushed. Like a lonely lady lost in a solemn garden of her own making. A wraith instead of a human being.

"Two hours . . ." Hanson echoed tonelessly. Suddenly, he shucked his officer's jacket, draped it over a chair and found a deck of playing cards somewhere. He began to clear the desk, motioning her to a chair. She watched him, once again liking the wise, alert movements of his lithe figure.

"But I worry a great deal about you, Chris," she insisted in her mellow voice. "What ever happens to me, I earned. Married women with families and consciences . . . shouldn't."

It was as if he hadn't been listening. "Sit down, Laura." He drew the chair closer to the desk.

"You're expecting strength from me," she protested softly. "You may not get it. I'm not sure I have the strength you need."

He reached across to her, setting her in the chair almost forcibly. She appeared ready to continue her apology. He tightened his hands on her arms, pushing his face close to her own.

"Laura, hang on to hope with . . . both hands. The proof you're looking for is all in a steel box in what's left of the 'Adrianna.' I *know* it."

She nodded dumbly, trying hard to believe him. He could see that. He could also see that she had not been exaggerating, that her inner strength was a frail, delicate thing that could be toppled to dust with one last push of cruelty. And disappointment.

He pulled her closer, face to face, his own expression sober and earnest.

"Now listen to me." She nodded again. "Are you paying close attention?"

"Yes," she said very seriously.

"Five card draw," Hanson said without humor. "Jacks or better to open. *Nothing wild.*" Even as he accented the last two very meaningful words, he drew her closer, kissing her gently on the tip of her nose. "And for the next two hours, glorious ones I should think, we'll try to forget the last miserable year."

A halting smile crossed her lovely face fleetingly. She sat back in her chair, clasping her hands across the table top. Hanson began to shuffle the cards, riffling them with the expertise of long, long hours sitting here to while away the time of lonely sea voyages. She understood that about him too.

They exchanged glances.

Hanson dealt, whisking out the five cards to each of them with brisk, deft speed. The quiet restfulness of the quarters which Douglas Rigby had liked so much was tranquil and at peace. Laura Travis felt one moment's freedom and happiness.

It was like Thomas Hardy's novel. So like that.

Far from the madding crowd . . .

Herself and Chris.

Alone and together.

So unlike the terrible place she had just come from.

On the second day out, with the crew still pondering the enigma of the blazing lights of the night before, Leoncavallo Borghese, consciously avoiding the company of his father, Giovanni, was wandering aimlessly midships when he first heard the curious sound. It was a rhythmical, resonant clapping noise. The sound one could manufacture by slapping two strips of hollow wood together. Intrigued, he sought out the source of the sound. It was not very far away.

His steps led him to the bow of the vessel. There in the bright light of day, he was treated to a spectacle he would not have dared to imagine aboard a tramp steamer such as the *Batavia Queen*. The sight warmed his heart.

Appreciatively, he drew nearer.

The four Japanese girl divers, piquant and very attractive in their colorful sarongs, were performing a curious dance. This seemed to be an arrangement whereby the dancer had to step deftly and delicately between and over bamboo sticks manipulated to come together with steady, unbreaking tempo. The most charming of the divers was maneuvering snakily and sensually between the sticks, eluding them even as she performed a rhythmic island dance. Leoncavallo was drawn to her. The laughing face, the raven black hair, the fine young womanly body. This was Toshi, the leader, who had blessed the *Batavia Queen* in the presence of her captain. Her companions were Midori, Sumi and Kiko. The laughing, happy Oriental girls, unaware of Leoncavallo, romped and cavorted between the sticks. Toshi, graceful and managing the intricate, hazardous-appearing steps before any of them could touch her, had her back to the young Italian. Kiko, smiling and kneeling with one of the poles that attempted to trap Toshi before she could elude it, spotted Leoncavallo. Abruptly, her smile faded and she stopped moving her pole. The dancing jarred to a halt. Toshi paused in bewilderment. Then she saw Leoncavallo, and realizing she and her friends had been watched, her happy expression dissolved and her eyes clouded over. Leoncavallo grinned broadly at her, to no avail. She marched directly toward him, her head high and defiant. Her lips trembled.

"If you please, sir, our captain has told us to consider this part of the ship as ours." Her head lowered in sudden embarrassment. "Not to be watched and laughed at." Her three friends, hanging back, matched her hangdog expression.

"I wasn't laughing at you, believe me," Leoncavallo murmured with ingratiating truth. "What game is that?"

Toshi looked up at him blankly. Immediately, he described what he meant, duplicating the clapping together of the bamboo poles.

She didn't understand. Leoncavallo tried again, completely conscious of the fact that she was a hauntingly breathtaking girl. So different from any of the women he had known. So unlike Francesca. She was like a breath of spring.

"The"—he clapped his hands again—"game."

She nodded quickly then, comprehending.

"It's tinikling." She spoke with a pronounced but rather delicate accent. "From the Philippines."

"May I try?"

"It would not interest you."

"I'd like to try. May I? Please?"

She hesitated. His appeal was undeniably sincere. Leoncavallo smiled, took her hands and led her gingerly toward the extended bamboo poles still held by the other girls. She recoiled slightly from his touch but allowed him to continue. Her friends smiled now and began to pick up the three-beat clump-clump-clack rhythm of tinikling. Leoncavallo placed his right foot tentatively between the scissoring rods, withdrawing it before the sticks clacked together. Toshi watched him for a solemn moment and then quickly stepped into a momentary opening to meet him face to face. The sticks clacked and clumped. She placed her small hands on his shoulders. He was quick to do the same. Now, at arm's length, they moved through the simple, first steps of the dance. Leoncavallo followed her lead. It was difficult keeping his eyes and mind on the movement of his feet. Toshi was too close. Too soft and warm and desirable.

"My name is Leoncavallo Borghese," he blurted over the noise of the sticks coming together with hollow impact.

She set her mouth, forming the name carefully.

"Leon–cava–loo."

He laughed. Happily, boyishly. She smiled apologetically. He began to correct her, suddenly thought better of it and stared at her levelly, even as their feet avoided the clacking, clumping bamboo poles.

"That is wonderful, really. It sounds better your way."

"You are kind," Toshi whispered.

They held on to one another with their eyes while their legs described the steps of tinikling.

To Kiko, Sumi and Midori, the actions of Toshi were as clear as the rainbows over the rice paddies of Japan. They had never seen her give her hands to any man. Smiling among themselves as women will who share a secret, they continued to beat out the happy love story of tinikling.

Oblivious to them, to the beating bamboo poles and to the slight pitch of the deck of the *Batavia Queen*, Leoncavallo Borghese and the Japanese diver called Toshi Namura danced on.

Had Giovanni Borghese been present to see, he would have been the first observer to note the remarkable change in his only son. He might have been astounded.

For the first time in months, Leoncavallo was happy.

Laura Travis sat in her bunk, staring moodily into space. She had long since lost interest in the open book on her lap. She found it difficult to concentrate on anything for longer than a few moments. Her mind was a riot of doubt and despair with long intervals of solemn reverie. She had made up her mind to get hold of herself but it wasn't easy. Indeed, it was a veritable chore. The ghosts of the past and the future were cavorting fearfully in her imagination. She was as much at sea as the *Batavia Queen* was. Yet the vessel had a charted course, a destination, a purpose. Laura Travis felt like flotsam, washed haphazardly along at the mercy of all things. It was a dreadful way to feel.

A sound, a rustling hiss of paper, caught her attention. Her eyes swung toward the cabin door. There she spied the white corner of a stationery-size sheet of paper lying in view, protruding from the frame of the barrier. Quickly, she scrambled from the bunk to crouch on the floor to retrieve it. In hasty, crude lettering, a penciled message greeted her eyes: *"The cook is very sad."* Before she could solve that small mystery, there was another rustle of sound and a matching note slid under the door. This one read: *"No dinner last night, no breakfast today."* She started to smile, realizing the playful quality of the notes. Too, at the bottom of the second message was a hastily sketched circle with eyes and a turned-down mouth. Before she could straighten, a third note joined the first two. *"You could make this cook very happy."* The same moon-faced sketch now appeared with the mouth turned up in a smile. Now Laura Travis really smiled. A fourth note, a final piece of paper, slid under her gaze. "FOR FURTHER DETAILS OPEN DOOR." She complied, still smiling, temporarily rescued from her dismal mood.

Hanson was standing in the corridor, looking trim and handsome and neat in his uniform. He lounged against the door frame.

"I'm depending on you this evening," he said almost commandingly. "My hostess—beautiful, gracious, serene—*smiling*. Eight bells sharp."

"Oh, Chris—"

"You *will* be beautiful, gracious, serene and smiling, won't you?"

"You fool."

"That is not an answer."

"I'll be . . . prompt anyway."

"Perfect."

He moved as if to pull the door closed but hesitated.

"And smiling?" He grinned.

She nodded, genuinely amused, and turned toward her wardrobe. Hanson had one last enjoinder. Poking his head in once again, he asked, "And maybe a *little* bit gracious?"

Laura Travis finally laughed out loud at that. Hanson ducked back out, closing the door. And her laugh and smile faded into the sad mold of before. The expression went out like a candle.

In the corridor, Hanson frowned.

It would take time, he could see that.

Poor Laura. She had endured so much in so little time. Unsmiling, he hurried down the corridor, finding the deck stairs almost without seeing them. He took them, two at a time, going up. There had been a storm threat on the western horizon according to the last watch. He meant to avoid as much foul weather as possible.

He headed for the bridge, trying not to think about how much he wanted to fold Laura Travis in his arms for a long kiss that might help blot out the tragedies of the past.

She looked so damned tired and *defeated*.

He wondered if she would ever tell him what had really happened to her.

You could never tell with a woman.

Any woman.

The sky was darkening, and with this ample demonstration of Mother Nature's mighty hand casting long, irregular silhouettes across the bows of the ship, Harry Connerly yielded to his curse. Affording himself the cover and concealment of a tarpaulin-bound lifeboat, he extracted a small green bottle from the folds of his jacket. Tilting his head back, mindful of the glow from the row of open engine room skylights, he quickly sipped from the tiny neck of the bottle. He shuddered briefly and shook his head. For a long moment, he expelled a heavy sigh of relief.

It was only then that he was aware of Lester Danzig, the convict. From behind his back, a clumping sound and a rattle of the embracing leg chains warned him. Connerly turned slightly, finding himself face to face with the smiling, bearded face. Danzig's fiery, slitted eyes seemed to glow in the gloom.

"We're both wearing irons of a sort, aren't we?" Danzig said in an easy, friendly voice.

Connerly stared at him coldly. "Are we?"

He moved off a few paces, staring down into the engine room. The pound and staccato, rhythmic pump of the machinery came up to the deck with a contained frenzy of muted thunder.

Danzig watched him closely. "How long you been workin' with busted lungs?"

Connerly fixed him with an unwavering, still unfriendly stare.

"You got enough to do wearing leg chains without worrying about my insides."

Danzig shrugged. "The way I look at it, you're about the only fella above decks that's in anywhere near as bad shape as me."

This seemed to amuse the convict; he chuckled half-aloud and moved closer to Connerly. The burly diver let him come on, a bit amused himself.

"Worse maybe," Danzig continued in a low, unhurried tone. "That laudanum's bad stuff, friend. Anything that loaded with opium . . . well . . . one time I saw a fella who was takin' that stuff pick up an axe. A regular, double-bitted thing and—"

"You don't miss much, do you?" Connerly allowed himself a small smile.

"I've seen a lot of those little green bottles before. So's Hanson."

Connerly's expression tightened. He studied Danzig for a long moment. Danzig gestured reassuringly, his curious smile frozen on his long, angular face.

"Don't worry, friend. He won't hear it from Lester Danzig. How come you're still workin'? I've seen divers with better lungs than yours sweepin' streets to keep from havin' to go down again."

Harry Connerly gazed somberly across the darkened ocean.

"I've still got one good shot left."

"You sure picked a pippin."

The remark was offered with such authority that Connerly searched the convict's face for the answer.

"Why?"

"You coulda picked one with better odds."

"Hanson seems to know what he's doing."

"Fine."

"He's no fool, Danzig."

"Sure. Anyway, go light on those little green bottles, eh?" Danzig turned to go. A powerful arm and a hand the seeming size of an anvil fastened on his bony shoulder. Danzig winced. Connerly was glaring into his face now but showing no rage.

"You were going to say something."

A twitch contorted Danzig's face. But he grinned and poked a thumb at his own thin-lipped gash of a mouth.

"My biggest problem. All mouth. Forget it."

"I've got too much riding on this job," Connerly warned him harshly. His grip tightened and the spasm of Danzig's face widened. "What were you going to say?"

"Hanson'll heave me right back into that forward hold," Danzig protested. His attempt at a placating laugh was a dismal failure of sound.

"Like you said," Connerly reminded him. "He won't hear it from me. Now—" His face hardened. Danzig tried to pull away. But the remorseless hand pinned him like a fly. Connerly's determined, lined face loomed before his frightened eyes.

"Honest," Danzig quavered. "I give you my word—"

"Sure you do," Connerly said bitterly. "And I'm going to take it."

He twisted his arm, his shoulder bent forward and Lester Danzig blurted with fear and pain. The silhouettes of both men were limned starkly against the lights of the open engine room windows. Briefly, they struggled, reeling in a curious little dance of combat. Suddenly, Connerly released his hold and Danzig fell back against a bulkhead.

"Now we understand each other, don't we?" Harry Connerly said.

Lester Danzig could only nod dumbly, his slitted eyes batting furiously. His leg chains clanked hollowly.

His muttered affirmative, if there was one, was lost in the low muted pounding of the engine room.

Harry Connerly smiled.

A smile that is usually found on a death's-head.

The fancy salon where the Borgheses had had their important dart game now boasted the full complement of the individuals who had joined together in the curious expedition that was to make the name of the *Batavia Queen* legendary in the annals of the Java Sea. Captain Chris Hanson had invited all to the table for dinner. He was pleased with the turnout, especially since Laura Travis had finally surrendered her gloom to his brightness and appeared in the dining salon. She never looked lovelier in his memory. Her dark hair, piled in two shoulder-length coils, hung attractively down her shoulders, glowingly framed against her exquisite garb of Spanish lace and tight bodice above a flowing skirt. She looked more the madonna than ever. He was proud of her appearance, the quiet classicism that attended her every move and gesture. The slight inclination of her head seemed to throw her entire aspect into one of thoughtful divinity.

The Borgheses, father and son, attired in their Florentine best, single-breasted suits of long frock coats and matching trousers, neatly enhanced by wide black ties, were two of a kind. They seemed to have reached some sort of truce, Hanson noted. The father was calm, quiet and courtly as ever. Leoncavallo, the boy, even emanated a rare glow of vitality. Hanson had not missed how his eyes had kindled at the sight of Toshi Namura. The Japanese diver, piquant and as vibrant as any bird of paradise, was altogether stunning in her tightly bound sarong. She had even inserted a hibiscus flower in her raven tresses. Her eyes were deep and inscrutable. Yet she had a strange and intimate smile for the younger Borghese.

Douglas Rigby, yellow thatch of hair studiously combed, his tropical suit of white announcing his British Empire membership as blatantly as any unfurled Union Jack, was trying to maintain the detached, scientific air. But his youth and native enthusiasm were still defeating him. In time, Hanson knew, these two imperishable qualities might transform into pomposity and jadedness, but he hoped not. Still, he had seen it happen to even better men than Douglas Rigby.

As for Charley Adams, Hanson could only once again marvel at the sheer naturalness and vivacity of the young woman. She was one of those rare people, obviously, who remain the same in the face of all social change and disorder of being. She had done her golden hair into a bun behind her head and her tall, erect figure seemed designed for the lavender dress she wore. Miss Adams' eyes, which always smiled, and the laugh that was never very far from her wide and generous mouth were a tonic all in all. Hanson sensed that when the chips were down, Charley Adams might be worth two men.

He wished devoutly he was that certain of her consort, Harry Connerly. For openers, Mr. Connerly, for all his vaunted reputation as a deep-sea diver, was the first to evince signs of rebellion and shilly-shallying, as soon as Hanson led the group to the large deal table in the center of the salon.

Here, a baize-covered top held a large unfolded map. It was Hanson's plan to discuss the expedition immediately before inviting his guests to sit down to the lavish and very special meal he had ordered from Cook. The ship's gallery had been a whirlwind of activity all afternoon as Captain Hanson had sent down the decree. He wanted an outstanding table this night, thanks to the promised presence of Laura Travis.

The atmosphere of the salon was pleasant and extremely comfortable. The ship was riding easily, the crystal chandeliers barely tinkling with sound, and with everyone formally attired, the occasion was a potential social success. Only Connerly with his battered, billed cap, loosely buttoned shirt and rumblingly voiced objections, was the spoilsport. A weather-beaten killjoy who saw doom and disaster at every turn. Hanson was very surprised at that. The Connerly he had heard spoken of in whispers of awe in every Singapore saloon had apparently undergone some mammoth change of personality. And creed.

He was pounding the map on the baize cloth of the table, rustling the folds of the chart. His red face wore an expression of the utmost complexity. Mingled rage, fear and hostility.

"So I say we turn back," he exploded. "You never said anything about all these risks!" With that, he wheeled from the table, turning his back on everyone in the salon.

Toshi Namura, her placid face troubled, spoke softly to Hanson.

"Perhaps this has become too great a gamble for us now?"

Connerly came slamming back at that, glaring at Hanson across the table. As if he would scorn a man who was wearing his officer's regulation black uniform while he chose to dress casually.

"You shoulda told us, Hanson." There was reproof in his voice.

"I didn't tell you," Hanson said sharply, "because it's none of your business."

Giovanni Borghese, ever the smooth gentleman of manners, rowed calmly into the troubled waters.

"Captain Hanson. Permit me. If Mrs. Travis is indeed not fit, if her information—the information we depend on in risking our time and our lives—*is* doubtful, why, of course, it concerns us." He waved a broad arm to include everyone in his opinion.

For once, Leoncavallo Borghese seemed in complete accord with his parent. His earnest face and tone, half-apologetic, broke in.

"Certainly she told you there are pearls . . . but now we know she spent the last year in St. Margaret's. A mental institution."

"Laura Travis," Hanson said, "didn't hire you. I did."

Connerly snorted. "How do you know she didn't dream up the whole thing?"

Laura Travis, who had somehow drifted toward the rear of the salon, as if to detach herself from the discussion revolving about her name and her sanity, now turned back to face the group. Hanson studied her, his heart beating faster. She was idly touching one of the dangling jade earrings she wore as if it had suddenly become a hazard.

Connerly hesitated, torn between his innate goodness and the agony buffeting his consciousness. His tone and manner softened and he smiled at Laura Travis, motioning her forward. She glided easily into the heart of the group again. Hanson waited, certain she could handle the situation.

"Mrs. Travis," Connerly mumbled. "Were there pearls on your husband's ship?"

There was an almost electric silence. Hanson, tempted to say something, compressed his lips. Laura Travis stared back at Harry Connerly with a directness that was quite a thing apart from boldness. The other women in the room, Toshi and Charley Adams, sensed that difference, too. Nothing but candor and honesty would ever come from this lady.

"I don't know, Mr. Connerly."

A unified gasp of dismay raced around the room. As if unaware of the uncertainty of her disclosure, Laura continued, "Captain Hanson thinks there are."

"*Thinks* there are," Giovanni Borghese echoed quietly. There was a great sadness in his tone.

Laura Travis read his response and the feelings of the rest of them. With slow resignation, she started for the dining room door. Hanson quickly rescued the situation.

"*Knows*, Mr. Borghese." There was the steel of the ship's captain in Hanson's words. "Laura, stay where you are. Captain Travis had a sort of tradition, ladies and gentlemen. On his son's birthday each year"—he looked at Laura Travis—"he gave you a pearl. Do you have them with you?"

She hesitated. He smiled. A kind smile with his love all there.

"Yes," she said.

"Show them."

From somewhere on her person, she produced a very small embroidered bag. Just large enough to retain keepsakes or treasured items. In this case, it proved to be seven pearls.

Hanson took one of them from her, rotating it between his thumb and forefinger so that his selected group of adventurers and specialists could measure its true beauty and value. The glow of the suspended crystal chandeliers reflected the light of a million stars. The flickering oil lamps, burning steadily, captured the radiance, too.

The group flocked about Hanson, crowding him, reveling in the exposed pearl. Hanson, smiling grimly, placed the tiny concentration of wealth and splendor on the baize cloth of the table. It rolled slowly across the material. Toward Toshi Namura. She caught it before it could fall to the floor. She looked at it quickly, appraisingly. Douglas Rigby said, "By George!" and immediately hushed up, as if embarrassed. Toshi Namura, her Oriental calm dissolving, restrained a gasp of awe.

"You're an expert," Hanson said. "What's it worth?"

The girl was visibly astonished. "Only twice in my life have I seen a pearl like this. It is *very* valuable."

"And hundreds of them would be worth—?"

"Would be worth a fortune," Toshi Namura concluded.

Hanson nodded. "That is one pearl out of a shipment the 'Adrianna' was carrying. There are ten packets more two days from here. Gentlemen . . ." He gazed at the Borgheses, Douglas Rigby and Harry Connerly. "It's worth a trip, isn't it?"

The pearl was passing from hand to hand, with varying expressions of amazement and interest. Connerly was the last to hold the treasure in his rugged hand. Hanson was watching the elder Borghese. Borghese Senior contemplated for only a second longer and then nodded his head in the affirmative.

"Yes," Giovanni Borghese murmured.

Hanson's eyes rested on Harry Connerly. It was obvious where the others stood; Rigby could not be contained, the Italians would function as a unit and the women would follow their men. He spoke for Laura Travis, of course, and Toshi Namura would do her sworn duty. But what of Connerly? Charley Adams would do whatever he wanted, certainly.

"I don't know," Connerly said, still holding the pearl.

He glanced at Laura Travis, looked at the pearl again and rolled it across the table top. He rolled it toward Hanson who merely kept staring at him.

"I guess," Connerly said, wagging his head but not at all decisively, "I got nothin' else to do."

Turning, he walked out of the salon, his wide shoulders

hitching as he shrugged. Charley Adams murmured something in a low voice and followed him. Hanson sighed, relieved. The temporary ordeal was over. You had to start an expedition with all hands in agreement or else there was disaster. He tugged a pocket watch from a uniform pocket, smiling easily at the others. "Dinner is *supposed* to be at—"

Before he could state the time, a metallic, siren-like scream of noise filled the salon. It rapidly amplified to a deafening, ear-splitting shriek. The group in the salon reacted with duplicate intensity, clapping their hands over their ears, wincing, looking around in wonder and sudden fear at the startling interruption. The chandeliers tinkled warningly. The oil lamps began to sputter. A cold wind seemed to fan across the salon. Toshi Namura closed her eyes, her lips forming a soundless prayer.

Hanson bit his lip and dashed for the stairs leading up to the bridge. The thunderous volume of the banshee wailing seemed to emanate from the very walls of the salon.

Even more incredibly, inexplicably, the *Batavia Queen* had begun an unaccountable rocking motion. The very boards beneath Hanson's feet were pitching dangerously.

There was no excuse, no nautical explanation for that.

None at all.

In the wheelhouse Jacobs frowned at the helmsman on duty. The violent level of sound had increased to a mind-deadening scream of pure high frequency. It was coming from all directions, surrounding, overwhelming the *Batavia Queen*. The answer to the enigma was not to be found in the quiet, darkened sea. The ship was rocking gently, as if in the clutch of a gathering communion of the waves. Jacobs, in a mild panic facing the unknown but still sure there was a proper seaman's answer for all things, snatched up the speaking tube, ringing the boiler room.

"We got a boiler blowing?" he barked into the tube.

In the sweaty, steam-filled boiler room the grease-smeared men stood about in confusion, their eyes searching the upper levels for some answer. Driscoll, the engine room chief, as puzzled as everyone else, answered the query sounding from the tube on the bridge. It was hard to hear above the keening wail of noise.

"No, it ain't a boiler, Mr. Jacobs."

The seamen milling about him were gape-mouthed with wonder.

On the shadowy deck, Hanson had been joined by Laura Travis and the others. The sound, still pulsating and reverberating, carried across the waters. No lights other than stars shone in the skies. Hanson swiftly climbed the bridge ladder to the wheelhouse. The damned ghostly wailing seemed to be the only sound in the universe. It was awesomely tangible and yet unseen. Unknown.

Down in the prisoners' hold there was a frantic stirring, a terrified mass rattling of manacles and leg irons. Hysteria swept among the refuse and dregs of humanity. This was the topmost measure of discomfort and unreality. This insane, high-pitched, caterwauling agony of sound that made the horrible hold even more of a cross to bear. There was a great lashing of chains, a concerted moan of despair. The burly guard was having his hands full in restoring order, but even he knew how the prisoners felt. A clammy sensation of dread made his uniform cling to his flesh.

"Quiet down," he growled feebly. "Or it'll go even harder on you pigs!"

On the aft deck, Lester Danzig swayed against a bulkhead, hands cupped to his ears. For a moment his slitted eyes showed their shock and disbelief.

Jacobs and the on-duty helmsman made room for Hanson in the wheelhouse. "Stop the engines!" Hanson ordered. Almost on the command, the engines shut down with one abrupt stutter of sound. The captain swept on, out to the port bridge. He stationed himself at the rail, listening. His entire manner was one of complete alertness. A stifled oath erupted from his throat.

The sound had mysteriously, suddenly vanished. It was gone. Not even a ripple of echo lingered over the dark seas. Baffled, Hanson scanned the far horizon. To no avail. As with the mysterious dazzling lights of the night before, this new phenomenon had also disappeared. Going as quickly and amazingly as it had come.

Douglas Rigby spoke from somewhere behind Hanson. In the youthful scientist was still that unfrightened, all-interested intellect which had seen and heard phenomena and somehow reveled rather than recoiled.

"What do you think, Captain?"

Hanson turned easily. His eyes smiled, despite the new and great uneasiness that lay upon him in the face of mysteries for which a sea captain must have answers—if he is to survive.

"I think we should go back and finish dinner."

Neither of them saw Harry Connerly lurching against the

rail on the aft deck. Connerly, who had had such an agonizing time during the strange sound assault that he hadn't even had time to consider it or be frightened. The small green bottle of laudanum had been gulped from again and again. Through a haze of agony and torment, Connerly was scarcely aware of the shrieking sirens of the night. It all seemed part and parcel of his condition. His usual condition. One of disorientation and mental misery. He had had to hang on to his own sanity in a vortex of pain that always positioned him in its very center. He struggled to right himself against the superstructure of the ship. Waves of pain rolled over him.

The light patter of a woman's footsteps behind him suddenly sounded more sharply and clearly than anything else in the last awful minutes. He straightened, raising the green bottle up in a gesture of defiance.

"Are you sick, Harry?" Shrillness and fear were now in Charley Adams' warm voice.

"I hope to hell I'm sick." He pushed out his hands. "I wouldn't want to feel like this and be well." The attempt at humor made him cough. Charley touched his arm gently.

"Harry."

He raised the laudanum bottle to his lips to take another swig.

"Harry, I know you're in pain, but please go easy on that stuff."

"Charley," Connerly mumbled, "we don't know if those pearls are where that woman says. We don't know if the wreck is where it's supposed to be."

"Tell Hanson," she pleaded.

He shook his head grimly. "Tell Hanson nothin'! We need the money."

"Harry, we don't need the money that much. What if you have to go too deep?"

"Then I'll go as deep as I have to. I don't wanta talk about it."

"Harry, listen . . . you're just gonna hurt yourself."

"Will you let me alone, Charley?"

"No!"

He stared at her for a short hard moment, still swaying. Still racked with stabbing knives. He shook his head and stumbled away from her, past all argument.

Charley Adams watched him go, her eyes filling with tears of mingled love and anger. Not even her normal terror, springing up wildly at first hearing of the weird banshee sounds that filled the night, could equal the gnawing dread that tore at her insides every time she saw Harry Connerly dip into the questionable mercies of the little green bottle.

It was like watching the slow steady death of a proud, brave man. A strong man. The strongest.

The little truth that she loved that man only made the watching harder. She knew Harry Connerly was heading for the Deep Six, the irrevocable end to all things in life, and she was powerless to stop his insane journey.

It would have been simpler for her to hold back the mighty seas with her two slender hands.

Love can move mountains but it can't stop anyone from dying.

The use of laudanum has its penalties. Though it took Harry Connerly's pain and dissolved it into dead masses of muscles and reflexes, it opened his mind and his eyes to nightmare. The terrors and horrors of a man's life could be brought more sharply into focus, made more vivid through the bountiful effects of a pain-reducing drug. For Harry Connerly, laudanum was a passport to hell on earth.

The journey into Bedlam took place in the chain locker room immediately after Connerly had left a weeping Charley Adams on deck. His dragging steps had somehow led him down into the room where his gear was stored. There among the equipment that enabled him to go to depths of the ocean where no other men had gone, he paused to wash his steaming face in a large wooden tub of clear water. With waves of agony still coursing over him, Connerly had resorted to the little green bottle once more. When he finally replaced the laudanum in his pocket, the damage to his mind had been completed. He was ripe for nightmare. The chain locker room, with its fantastic assortment of equipment, was a proper setting for hallucination.

A hanging oil lamp threw a dim, iridescent glow over the narrow compartment. Shadows thrown by the lamp seemed to climb slowly up and down the bulkheads, dancing fitfully with every roll and plunge of the ship. The organized disarray of coiled hawsers, cable clamps, tackles, blocks, canvas, sailing supplies and general stowage was an army of friends yet somehow strangers in the night. Harry Connerly blinked, the dousing water still running down his beetled face. He stood in the middle of the locker, the old-fashioned wooden bathtub at his feet, half-filled with water.

He was breathing tremulously. Closing his eyes, he shook

his tousled head violently. He blinked, squinted into the gloom. As everything in that room took form, evolved into shape, Harry Connerly's mind began the speedy descent into madness. And nightmare.

The locker room had tilted alarmingly. Distorted now, the lamp and the massed equipment took on separate, different identities. Everything in the room now seemed alive. Ominously alive and fraught with danger. The coiled anchor chains were undulating like a giant moray eel. The clamps and tackles were reaching out like the claws of monster crabs. The dangling lamp had become a hideous, leering evil eye of an ugly, wart-faced devil fish. The shadows were extending like a hungry, yearning octopus, all eight tentacles probing, searching for the man called Harry Connerly.

He gaped; his tongue clove to the roof of his mouth. All these things, all these objects that related to his life as a deep-sea diver, the fears he had suppressed, the unfathomable creatures of his imagination, had come to being. The laudanum had opened his eyes, sharpened his nerve ends again, made panoramic his view of life and death. The chain locker room crawled with his mental monsters. New, equally fearsome shapes and objects were coming into the focus of his fever dream. Colors had heightened, sounds had increased in intensity. There was a throbbing violence of noise in the room. The walls tilted some more, the devilish things and creatures closed in on him. He recoiled, trying to run, to hide. The bulkhead wall stopped him. He trembled, his hands two huge knots of fists. Hollow noises reached his ears—all the underwater whispers, echoes and clanking rhythms which a diver always hears. Now he could also hear the methodical wheeze of his air compressor as it sighed and gurgled into the lonely, dependent steel helmet fixed to his head. The sound of his past, plummeting a hundred feet into a cold dark sea.

Bubbles surrounded him, little life-saving globules of air.

This was how it is. How it was . . .

He clawed the bulkhead wall behind him, gasping for breath, his mind rioting. And still behind him, coming on relentlessly, remorselessly, was the transformed and metamorphosed equipment. The giant moray eel, the monster crabs, the one-eyed devil fish, the dark, inky octopus . . . and all the other nameless, horrible beasts that forever lurk in the human mind, needing only a drug to evoke them into being.

The locker room was a madhouse and he was caught in the very heart of the lunacy. A gibbering, crying, blubbering child of anguish. Afraid of the dark. Afraid of nightmare because it might all very well be true. . . .

The serpentine mass of anchor chains had closed in on Connerly. He recoiled, trying to twist from the enveloping arms. For a mad second his sanity tottered. His heart thundered and all the sounds of the sea life he knew cascaded down on him like tons of pouring water.

When the chain locker door opened inward, Connerly's gaze swung toward it mechanically. His dazed eyes, through a curtain of terror and confusion, saw the figure of a woman. A kimono-clad woman, carrying a wooden bucket over one arm. He could not read the friendly, pleasant smile on the face of one of Toshi Namura's diving girls. The girl crossed to the wooden bathtub, a wavering image in Connerly's gaze. He followed her dumbly, his ears trying to catch a clear sound, his mind still locked on the phantom monsters just beyond his back.

Connerly, still clutching his little green bottle, whimpered.

The girl, Kiko, shyly murmured, "Hello."

Connerly blinked, shook his head again.

"*Hello.*"

The greeting, reduplicated in his hallucination, echoed emptily in his ears. The girl, pouring the bathtub water now, was oblivious of him, unaware that her greeting had detonated a chain action of exploding bombs. *Hello–hello— hello–hello!*"

Connerly flinched, fixing a glare on the intruder. Her trim, pretty figure wavered, shimmered and fanned out into a large, deadly glob of fresh new terror.

Kiko's image weaved in and out of his consciousness like a wraith. Her smile seemed a loathsome thing; her black hair seemed to drift as it would undersea. Her presence was somehow obscene, murderous; she was like a creature dredged out of the depths of the hellish sea. A shape-changing malevolent that would soon become another monster to destroy Harry Connerly.

Fumblingly, he pocketed his little green bottle.

Anxiety was etched on the face before him. Kiko, knowing something was wrong with this bronzed man, did not know what that something was. True, there was something menacing about the man though he cowered as the men of the village did when mighty Krakatoa spoke. But Connerly's bulk in the shadows of the locker room and his cold, flinty eyes were dangerous to behold. Still, the compassionate heart of Kiko reached out to him.

"You all right?" she asked in her very limited English.

"Get away from me!" Connerly snarled, batting away her long, ugly tentacle.

"I help you . . ." She paused, confused, the bathtub water forgotten. The man was acting so strangely.

She took a step toward him, extending her hand.

To Connerly, it was a repellent tentacle out to destroy him.

Cursing, he threw himself at the tentacle. And at her.

She struggled, numb with fear, as his huge hands closed about her narrow waist. He shook her hard, pumping her up and down so that her long dark hair tumbled wildly down her shoulders. The kimono slipped, baring one soft, tumescent breast. She shuddered, her body shaking frantically. Connerly squashed her in his big arms, grinding his face into the hollows of her shoulders. His breath was a rasp of animalism. Sheer manpower and man-smell.

She raked at his brutish face with her fingernails. The pressure of his violent hands increased. She began to feel herself fading into darkness.

Suddenly, shrilly, she screamed.

The chain locker exploded with the force and ferocity of that scream. It bounded, clanged and volleyed a million echoes among the dreadful sea monsters encircling the twisting bodies of Connerly and the girl.

Again she screamed.

Connerly's mind came apart.

Whimpering, babbling incoherently, he bore Kiko down across a coil of stacked rope. His hands tore at her, fought the tresses, the loathsome smile. Whether the devils found him or not, by God, he was taking one of them with him.

They were still coming, too.

Three of them now, even as his own hands, pummeling and clawing, sought to drive the life out of the monster in his grasp. They were weaving toward him now. A blur of figures, misshapen and monstrous. Skeleton-dead faces peered at him from the faceplates of diving suits. Hooks protruded from the long rubber arms. The third figure was headless. No helmet was attached to the steel collar. He drew back, terrified, forgetting the limp monster beneath him. He kicked out, snarling.

The three figures swarmed over him. The two divers and the headless apparition. Connerly's enormous strength, heightened by the drug, drove them back. He swayed, breathing hard, trying to clear his eyes. He was dimly aware of the fallen monster, moving away, running from the chain locker. And then one of the newcomers brought a strip of heavy wood down on his head, and Harry Connerly swam crazily in a swirling sea of lights and noises and throbbing waves of pain. The sea monsters receded. The dim light stopped moving. The chain locker righted itself. His vision cleared.

The nightmare ended.

Harry Connerly, sprawled on the crowded floor of the locker room, looked up.

He squirmed to a sitting position. The aspects and horrors of his madness had all fled back into the dark labyrinth of his mind. He recognized all the gear and stowage equipment for what it was. The abyss had closed into a tight scar, with no yawning space between.

First Officer Jacobs and two of the ordinary seamen were standing over him. Staring down with contempt and hard-faced anger even as they nursed their collection of small bruises.

Jacobs looked very angry about something. Connerly did not know what that could be. What had Jacobs to do with him?

"Come on," Jacobs said in the sort of voice one used to smash insects that ran out from under rocks. "Get up. The captain'll be wanting to talk to you."

Connerly lurched to his feet, conscious only of a ringing pain under his scalp and a general sense of the utmost confusion.

What the hell had happened?

That he had to take guff from Hanson's first mate . . .

The cage was awkward, cumbersome.

It had heavy, closely grilled vertical slats. About five feet by two, it closely resembled an Oriental fish trap. In fact, the Oriental mind alone was capable of devising such an instrument of torture. The one euphemistically known as the Little Ease.

In the cage on the aft hatch, Harry Connerly was forced to squat in a hunched position. Half-standing, half-kneeling, his compulsory crouch made him seem like a tightly compressed foetus. The bars before him, gripped to hold himself even in this horrible way, underlined the discomfort of the cage. Fright and agony were etched on Connerly's bronzed face. The cage, swinging like a pendulum on a tight line falling from the mizzen mast, lashed to a swivel on the top center slat of the prison, was a jarring, bone-breaking ordeal. And now the blazing sun, burning down from on high, had heated up the cage to an almost unbearable point. Connerly's body literally baked. The bars of the cage burned against the palms of his hands. Like a bug in a box, hung high and dry to boil in the sun. And for what?

Away from his laudanum and his hallucinations, Connerly could only realize that Hanson had ordered such a summary punishment for the attempted rape of one of the Jap diving girls. That was a laugh. With a looker like Charley, what did he need with a little Jap girl? But—his clouded mind also told him—taking the laudanum must have left him a few pennies short in the memory department. What the hell could he have done that for? Unless it was those damn crawling things he saw in his wild dreams . . .

Poor Charley.

There she was. Far down below, it seemed like a million miles away, staring up at him and his damned cage. He didn't have to be right on top of her to know she'd be crying.

He stared down at the deck, seeing the world of a ship from a bird's-eye view. He could think of better ways of being on top of things. His back ached, his skin burned and his eyes were watering badly.

Hell, hell, hell. What a boat to get yourself in!

His thoughts roared on. Bitter, confused, still disoriented. Still not quite clear in his mind exactly what had happened to bring him to this sorry pass.

He also had no notion of what Hanson would consider a suitable punishment period. Six hours? Twenty-four? Two days? Three? Or the rest of the damned voyage. How the hell would he be worthwhile to dive if they battered him this way? Or didn't that matter anymore?

He could make out the lantern, bearded face of Lester Danzig staring up from below. The damned convict was right. Laudanum had ruined him all right. Good and proper. He might never be a whole man again.

He could also see how the rest of them were taking it.

The Italian showman, that Giovanni Borghese; you would have thought he had a ringside seat at a circus or something. Looking up. Interested. Not feeling sorry at all about a fellow human being in trouble. He could have sold tickets, you bet.

And that Rigby apple. The boy scientist. No doubt he had some great notions about this; like it was another experiment or some such. How long could a man last in the sun without food and water in such a lousy position?

He wasn't far wrong at that. Rigby and the Italian were exchanging notes. Only the son, the nice kid, wasn't looking up. He was staring down at the ocean from the starboard rail.

The Japanese diving girls were in a tight little cluster at the aft, huddling around one of their group. From Connerly's point of view, the raven-haired heads and little bodies looked like a floral arrangement.

There was Hanson and that Mrs. Travis, too. On the bridge. Standing still as statues. Connerly wondered what they were talking about. He had a feeling the woman would put in a word for him. Mental institution or not, she looked like a decent sort.

The Dutch guard in charge of prisoners in the hold was outside the engine room having a chat with Jacobs, the first officer.

Connerly suddenly hated the sight of Jacobs and the guard. They represented all the horror and unfairness in the world. He shook the bars of the cage bodily. It swayed in the high wind above decks, rotating slowly on the swivel.

Connerly glared at the burning sky, the limitless seas, the swarm of humanity below him. Down below, he did not see the Dutch guard fondling his heavy club nor did he see the patient, mute face of Jacobs, who simply reacted as a man who has seen everything—like Lester Danzig, who had also lived intimately with pain and whose own days were limited on the calendar.

The giant seaman Squid, still locked in the morbid memories of death on the sailing day, gazed up massively at the spinning cage. The great sorrow on the ebony face was eloquent. Had Connerly seen Squid he would have been happier in the knowledge that another human being shared his pitiful condition. Sympathized with it.

Squid lowered his gaze to see the man's woman, the golden-haired lady. The woman was crying. Squid's eyes roved, settling on the tiny Japanese woman, Kiko, who had somehow been the cause of this display of the captain's disfavor.

Charley Adams, unflinching but saddened more than she had ever been in her life, watched Harry Connerly sway helplessly in his cage of torture far above where she stood.

Now she lowered her eyes. Unable to look any longer.

On the bridge, Hanson sighed deeply. Regrettably. He had an abiding sympathy for all the actors in the little drama unfolding on the *Batavia Queen*. The weary, stale and turbulent lives of the passengers around him, locked to a swaying, precarious stage, elicited all his humanitarian instincts. Still, discipline was the strength of a ship. Its main strength. Without it, even armies toppled.

Laura Travis was as silent and immobile as a canvas painting. Only the drawn bow of her lips betrayed her.

Crushed by the slatted sides of his box-cage, Harry Connerly contorted, huddling like a small boy on the floor of his prison.

The sinful sun blazed down, bleaching the heart, the mind and the soul out of him.

The slow, easy movements of the *Batavia Queen* and the newly met anger of the sea, made the box-cage spin endlessly. First one way and then the other.

The Little Ease.

Connerly pondered that for a moment only.

Never had a Chinaman found a better name for anything.

Down on deck, Lester Danzig took a last look upward at Connerly before Squid sidled over to his side. Both men pushed away from the railing, disappearing forward. The giant's back rippled.

Four bells sounded.

Charley Adams was in the salon when Giovanni Borghese entered. He found the golden-haired creature tinkling with one finger on the handsome spinet situated in one corner of the lounge. Another of the rather curious captain's odd acquisitions. For a rough seafaring type, it certainly spoke volumes for a bit of breeding somewhere along the family line.

Borghese immediately went to Charley Adams' side and stared down at her. Speaking of breeding, he rather fancied the style and cut of this woman. A peasant, true, but of good quality and very decidedly *female*.

"I . . . ah . . . I would not presume to suggest that I know how you feel . . ."

She did not look up but continued her playing. A tuneless, discordant tapping of several keys in the alto side of the piano.

". . . but I sympathize."

Borghese picked up the empty glass on the piano head.

"I know . . . I *think* I know a little about people." He studied her profile. A trifle gross but still incredibly attractive. Lush, at the very least. "I have played over two hundred carnivals and from the height of my balloon, I have seen them all. People are confusing, are they not?" He paused, for she had nodded. "We put a label on this one or that, but—"

"Labels are for jam jars, Mr. Borghese," Charley Adams said, looking up quickly. "All my life I've been a singer. And with my kind of voice it's been mostly in saloons. Anyway, I can tell you firsthand—never put tags on people. The guys with clean collars and nice shiny faces pinch bottoms. The mean ones . . . the ones who *look* mean . . . they pinch, too. So don't tell me about labels. I've seen the one they put on Harry."

"People," Borghese said tactfully, "believe him to be a very violent man."

"*People* don't know Harry Connerly," she said bitterly.

"I am sure you are right. So now you sit here thinking, remembering all kinds of things. That he liked children, that he was kind to old ladies, perhaps—"

"To be honest, Mr. Borghese, I don't care if he kicks old ladies in the teeth . . . he's *good* to me." Her eyes went skyward. "And now they've got him in that cage like some kind of wild animal."

"Not for long, I am sure." Borghese felt a need to be kind. "This is just temporary, this—"

"Just until you need him, right?" The wryness in her was like a shaft of truth. Hitting home, on target. Borghese, unflustered, was, however, sincere.

"My sympathies are genuine, Miss Adams."

That softened her to the point of smiling through her concern. "Sure . . . I believe you."

"In a way," Borghese said reflectively, "he is a very fortunate man." This remark was accompanied by a slight, elegant and beautiful bow. With that, he took the glass and himself away from the spinet. Charley Adams returned to the keyboard and this time, instead of unharmonious notes, she began to play softly. From the far side of the salon, Giovanni Borghese cocked his head appreciatively.

Miss Adams was rendering, with great felicity unless his ears were deceiving him, the opening bars of "O Sole Mio." One of his favorite pieces.

The woman, apart from her obvious charms, was a fine pianist.

Borghese recognized her choice as a form of gratitude. He gestured airily for her to continue playing while he busied himself at the handsomely grained bar, making two drinks from Captain Hanson's ample stock.

Charley Adams caressed the keys, trying not to think of Harry aloft in his cage, cramped and hurt terribly, with the sweat pouring off him like water in that awful sun.

Poor Harry.

Lester Danzig, en route from the bridge deck onto the second deck and going aft toward the cabin ladder well, encountered Leoncavallo Borghese and Toshi, the Japanese diving girl. Danzig flattened himself against a bulkhead to permit them to pass. Leoncavallo flung him a glare and Danzig grinned back harmlessly. He smelled the fragrance of Toshi's hair as she swept past him. Danzig reflected only for a second on what the little Jap would feel like in a bunk and then dismissed the thought as unattainable. By that time he had gained the galley door. There he found a crewman, grimacing in the sun, holding on to the door for support. Danzig frowned.

The seaman smiled at him weakly.

"Hotter, or am I just imagining?"

Danzig did not slow down. He rasped an affirmation as he went by, fully aware that the temperature had soared as much as ten degrees in less than an hour.

"It's hotter."

He ducked into the stairwell, disappearing below. When he reached the crew's quarters, it was to interrupt quite a scuffle of sorts. Two of the crew, irritated and surly, were swinging wildly at each other. Danzig stepped between them as shouted cries from both parties claimed innocence from troublemaking.

"What's got into you two?" Danzig growled.

The seamen, petulant and blood-streaked faces, crying out complaints that had no foundation in anything other than the now fierce heat, gave Lester Danzig pause.

Judas Priest, it *was* hot.

And it was getting hotter every second. Now he was fully aware of the perspiration beading his forehead, running down his nose. It didn't make sense.

Danzig frowned even wider as he got the two sailors to go on about their business. What with all the odd things happening on board since they left Singapore, he had an acute feeling the *Batavia Queen* was somehow spooked.

A jinx ship, if he was any judge.

This feeling was shared to a great degree by Kuan who was standing at the large wall thermometer in the engine room. The systematic pumping of the engines had driven most of Kuan's crew to their knees, defeated by the twin discomforts of sound and stifling heat. Kuan could not believe his eyes as he made a mark on the wall beside the thermometer. His men lay sprawled about him, shirts soaked to the smallest inch of material. Kuan had made other marks since he came on duty but this last indication was inhuman. Kuan's smooth face was blank as he crossed to the speaking tube that connected to the wheelhouse.

He blew into the tube to clear it and issued the startling information: "I don't understand it. It's almost night and the temperature's going *up!*"

At the other end, Hanson stared dumbly at the tube. Then he shook himself, acknowledged Kuan's report and hooked the tube to the wall again. He shook himself, as if that gesture alone would invalidate Kuan's news. Frowning, he left the wheelhouse, acutely conscious of the blood-red rays of a sun dipping into the western horizon. Jacobs was leaning on the rail, staring interestedly down at the water. Hanson joined him.

"Another four degrees, Frank."

Jacobs nodded, pointing down. He didn't seem too surprised with the report from the engine room.

"Look down there. More of 'em. That's more than a hundred in the last twenty minutes."

Hanson stared in the indicated direction. His mind was racing furiously. Weird lights, ghastly noises and now this incredible reversal of normal weather processes.

Jacobs' report was just as gloomy and unfathomable.

The surface of the sea close to the *Batavia Queen*'s hull was saturated with the carcasses of countless fish. There was no mistaking that. When you saw the whites of their bellies and they moved slowly, at the whim of the currents, they were dead.

Hanson was oddly chilled by the sight. He shivered briefly in his sticky jacket. He turned and stared toward the mizzen mast where the infernal cage prison rotated dizzily above the deck, looking like some fantastic flying object against the darkening red of the sky.

Jacobs looked a question at his captain. His pocked, sullen face was curious.

"Take a look at Connerly," Hanson said.

Laura Travis moved along the companionway. The unbearable heat wave seemed to gather momentum and increase intensely with each forward roll of the ship. Not even the promise of nightfall had lessened the assault. She stopped in the passage, fumbling for a kerchief with which to blot her soaked temples and forehead. She had not realized she had halted before the open cabin door of Douglas Rigby.

She heard his voice before she saw him.

"I have a theory, Mrs. Travis."

She turned in surprise, finding herself opposite the door which stood ajar to reveal Douglas Rigby in all his youthful and scientific splendor.

He was sitting at a make-do desk, books and important-looking papers and documents before him. He pointed a long pencil at her. His white jacket was partially unbuttoned and his thatch of hair was lank with perspiration. Yet he seemed unaware of discomfort. His earnest smile was as expectant and interested as ever. The wall space that Laura could see beyond him was overrun with maps, charts, bits of paper crammed with tidy handwriting—the silent testimony of Rigby's preoccupation with all things scientific. He waved cheerfully at Laura, beckoning her in.

"A theory?" she repeated, moving inward like an automaton. The heat had stupified her, dulled her senses.

"It concerns the heat and all we've been experiencing around here. Would you like to hear it?"

She entered the room slowly, looking wonderingly about the tiny, absolutely jammed and littered room. Even his bunk was strewn with tomes and books, a globe, a large brass microscope; it was a veritable rat's nest of scientific periodicals. *Harper's* magazines and odds and ends of notes, data, theses and Lord only knew what. She smiled at him in amazement.

"Where do you sleep, Mr. Rigby?"

"Oh, well . . . on the floor, sometimes. Do sit down." He bounded from his chair, steering her into it while he chatted on with his usual quota of endless enthusiasm. He was a hard young man to sit on for long. Something even Chris Hanson must have noticed.

"They're all connected, you know. The heat, the dead fish, those remarkable lights on the horizon, the weird sound—the lot. All connected." He paused very cryptically and added, "Like so."

He had walked to the wall where among the suspended litter hung a bold, hand-drawn map. His finger moved, stopping at a large black dot which proved to be an island in the Sundra Strait. Laura watched him, liking his friendly, preoccupied air. The uncomfortable weather had no perils for him. He was so enveloped in knowledge and theory he reminded her of a rather encyclopedic teddy bear.

Rigby's smudged finger was moving from one dot to another. His excited voice reeled off a list of names. "Rykyak. Malim. Percat. *Krakatoa.*" His arm described a sweeping, inclusive gesture. "Some volcanic, some not, but all connected in an underground chain."

"But only Krakatoa is dangerous," Laura protested.

He corrected her gently. "Only Krakatoa is a powder keg. But the whole island chain is a fuse. The heat, for instance, is being generated right beneath us this very moment. The awful banshee shriek that nearly drove us all witless was underground pressure along here somewhere." He tapped the map close to the dot that pinpointed the island of Malim.

She eyed him closely. He seemed so positive, so sure.

"Have you told the others these theories, Mr. Rigby?"

He shook his head energetically. "Absolutely not. Might put them off the trip entirely."

"Then why are you telling me?"

"Thought it might help to know these happenings are quite explainable." He shrugged.

"And therefore not so frightening?" She smiled. A sad smile. "That is very thoughtful, but I'm not really worried about *those* things. . . ." She began to rise from her chair. Douglas Rigby checked her with a hand.

"Mrs. Travis, speaking of fear, are you afraid of height or closed in places, or anything?"

She was surprised at the question but answered simply.

"No."

"I am." His smile was rueful. "Claustrophobia. Isn't that preposterous?"

She was goggled-eyed at that. "And you go down in that steel . . . thing. . . ."

"Chamber pot, my father called it. I suppose I do it to fight the fear and because what I see under the water is so magnificent. That's why I'm here actually." He sighed. "The valuables in your husband's safe can make my marine experiments possible. So if we are blotted out while trying, it won't have been so pointless . . . for me."

Again, she marveled at his foolhardiness even while admiring his courage.

"Enclosed in that little bell. Under the circumstances, Mr. Rigby, wouldn't a man have to be the tiniest bit insane to do what you do?"

"I expect he would," Rigby answered cheerfully enough.

She moved to the door, sensing the discussion was over. There was little else to say to a man who had his eye on something no one else could quite see. Suddenly, she caught sight of the thermometer tacked to the wall. Next to it, Mr. Rigby had marked a red-lined graph which showed an alarming rising curve. Like a streak of blood. Laura Travis pressed her kerchief to her forehead, reminded of the fierce swelter she had temporarily forgotten.

"Mr. Rigby."

"Yes, Mrs. Travis?"

"What effect might this heat have on someone constantly exposed to it . . . for a considerable period . . . without relief?"

"I suppose we're talking about Mr. Connerly, aren't we?" His true reply to her query was something that hammered into her consciousness like the repeated blows of a cruel weapon. "Then I would think another day, perhaps less, and he'll be of very little use to us."

Laura Travis and Douglas Rigby exchanged glances. Hers had all the sorrows and hurts of the world in it, his had that puzzled incredulity that eternally wonders about man's inhumanity to man.

Justice, if there was any at all, should be left to the wisdom and mercy of the immutable laws of nature. Not to man, whom Douglas Rigby had found to be most fickle and untrustworthy in the larger scheme of things.

The blistering heat suffocated the environs of the *Batavia Queen*. The vessel seemed to heel and stagger in the heavy seas. The paint-flaked hull and the single stack curling smoke skyward looked sodden and lifeless on the waters. Nobody on deck stirred. It was as if the blanket of nightfall lying athwart the bows had brought it with a monumentally thick and strangling warmth. Except for the lazy tendrils of smoke, the ship might have been Coleridge's "painted ship upon a painted ocean." Sluggishly, with agonizing slowness, the *Queen* plowed dead ahead. When ship's bells sounded, they thinkled tinnily in the night, extra beats apart, for the hand that tugged the cord was tired and short of energy. A great miasma of discomfort entrapped the decks, cabins, quarters and rooms of the ship. Caught in a phenomenon not of its own making, and one that surpassed understanding, Hanson's proud vessel crawled helplessly along.

In the forward hatch, the Dutch guard was cursing the mutinous, complaining groans of the prisoners piled like driftwood in the dark hold. The canvas sleeves of his tropical uniform were soggy with perspiration. The convicts, thrashing about in the cruel heat, were rattling their chains, pounding their manacles. The sound was a rhythmic beat of protest, registering on the guard's tired and brutal intellect like the devilish thumping of jungle drums in the bush—the sort of insane music one always heard on the islands. The guard hated such sounds.

Growling, he tightened his paw on the black rubber truncheon slung at his waist and loomed threateningly over the forward hatch. He slammed the club down on the canvas-covered roof of the hold. "Shut up down there!" he bawled. The pounding, rattling rhythms echoed back even stronger. Accompanying the increase in volume of noise came the hoarse, derisive shouts of the convicts below. The guard snarled and rapped with the truncheon again, harder than before. The angry noises did not abate.

In desperation, the guard spotted a crewman passing by with a wooden bucket slopping water. Feverishly, he claimed the prize and marched back to the canvas-covered hold. Muttering into the darkness, he whipped back the tarpaulin and overturned the bucket, sloshing its contents down into the hold. There was a shocked and then grateful rush of shadowy forms in the gloom. Convicts vied to meet the falling liquid. A blow was struck. Someone cried out in pain. The guard leered, chuckling.

"Hot, are you?" he spat down into the hold. "Well, damn you all, so am I!"

The cries from below changed to pleas, blurted outbursts for more water. Grumbling, the guard cursed them once more and walked back to the rail. He looked about in the gloom of the deck for a rope with which to lower the bucket over the port rail into the sea.

It was one way, the only way really, to try to keep cool. Such heat as this could drive a man insane.

Like the French disease that men spoke of in the Legion. *Le cafard*. It could make a man's brain burn like the fires of Hades, as he slowly changed from a human being into a gibbering, raving lunatic. The Moroccan deserts could fry a man out of his skin.

The guard shuddered, thinking about it.

The atmosphere of the wheelhouse was beyond bearing. A fine sheen of moisture clung to every board and instrument in the small confined area. Hanson stood over a wooden bucket of water, wringing out a dirty towel. He wiped it across his taut, throbbing face, then wrapped it about his neck. The stifling clutch of the heat was overpoweringly strong. Hanson had never experienced anything like this in all his years at sea. He could swear that Jan, the helmsman, hadn't either.

The poor man was a drenched mockery, his uniform was pasted to his body, stuck tightly at every joint.

Equipped with the mercifully damp towel, Hanson replaced him at the wheel. Properly relieved, Jan fled immediately to the wooden bucket to repeat his captain's performance, relieving himself of his jacket as he went. Hanson took the wheel. He mopped the sweat from his brow, silently damning the infernal weather conditions that had dogged him and his ship since weighing anchor in Singapore.

Laura Travis suddenly was in sight on the starboard bridge. Hanson waved at her breezily, despite his inner emotions. She managed to look as madonnalike and beautiful as ever, even though he was well aware of the limp folds of her dress.

"Welcome to West Purgatory," Hanson said.

"Chris . . ." She came forward, her hands clasped together to control some form of nervousness. He could see that, too. "You have to bring him down. We've discussed it. Harry Connerly can't survive in this heat. You really must—"

Charley Adams swung into the wheelhouse. Her face was tear-streaked and her lip rouge was awry. Hanson looked at both women and tried not to lose his temper. A captain had to maintain control of himself as well as a ship.

"Just a minute, Laura," he snapped. "*We've* discussed it. We are operating this ship by committee now?"

Her eyes clouded.

"I'm sorry, what I meant . . ."

"Am I permitted a vote under these new rules? Half a vote?"

Charley Adams interrupted, her voice underlined with worry and fear. "Harry'll be no help to you if you leave him up there."

Hanson turned to her, shaking his head.

"I'm not sure how much more of his *help* I can afford, Miss Adams."

Her tone and manner became desperate. Hanson saw the red rims of her eyes.

"Harry made me promise not to tell you this, Mr. Hanson, but he's in such awful trouble that . . ." Her voice trailed off, unable to continue.

"Then don't tell me."

Jacobs ducked into the wheelhouse, and from behind the backs of the two women, he nodded firmly to Hanson. He accepted the signal and pressed his hands to his damp jaws tiredly.

"But . . . but . . ." Charley Adams was at the end of her

rope. "I don't know what to do . . . I got no choice. . . ."
She was blurting now, a far cry from the easy, self-assured
woman of the days gone by. She began to sob convulsively.
Hanson went to her and Jan quickly darted in from the port
side bridge to protect the helm.

"Miss Adams," Hanson said softly, "we just brought him
down. He's waiting for you below."

She blinked at him through her tears. Then a grateful
smile broke through. Charley Adams was beyond coherence.
She whirled and ran from the wheelhouse. Laura Travis
turned a radiant smile on Hanson.

"Thank you, Chris."

"For what?" he retorted sourly, still angry with her. "For
knowing where my best interests lie? Forget it."

"I don't want to," she said.

"Suit yourself."

There would be time enough later to discuss things with
her. Not now. Not when this incredible heat wave was wearing everyone's nerves down to the breaking point.

The heat.

It had to break sometime.

It *must*.

Meanwhile, at least, Harry Connerly was out of the worst
part of it.

For a time the only sound in the wheelhouse was the sloshing noises that Jan was making at the water bucket.

It seemed like the only sound in the world.

Harry Connerly lay sprawled like a dead man on his bunk.
A wet cloth was placed across his weather-beaten forehead.
The big man looked helpless and forlorn in his unconsciousness. For Charley Adams, it was as if he had gone away and
might never come back. Not the old Harry, at any rate.

She wrung out another towel in the washbasin by his bunk
and carefully mopped at his beamlike arms, traveling the
cloth to his corded neck and shoulders. Charley's own face
was a damp mask of pain. Only her eyes held the withdrawal
from terror and pain which Hanson's decision had afforded
her. Thank God for a man like that.

Connerly suddenly stirred restlessly in his delirium. She
paused with the cloth until he subsided. His flesh was scalding to the touch of her fingers. Poor Harry. The sun had fired
him up like a boiler.

She straightened and walked slowly to the porthole window. She stared out into the muggy hell of the night. There was nothing visible. Not so much as a small star in the sky. Her body and her eyes ached.

But she was oddly elated, all the same.

Harry Connerly, her man, had been brought back from a living death. That was all that mattered now. Not pearls beyond price, not sunken treasures, not a world full of cheats and liars. To hell with mankind.

Sighing, she drifted away from the porthole, took one last look at Connerly and quietly left the cabin, closing the door softly.

His bronzed, beaten face with its mop of red, shingly hair might have been cast from metal. He looked so much like a god when he was sleeping.

Her God, and to hell with everyone else's.

Trouble was, God or not, he was also very much like a small boy sometimes.

Her boy.

On the chart table in his cabin, Hanson had set up a phonograph machine with the intention of repairing it. Laura Travis had discreetly knocked and he had let her in. There was much to talk about. Hanson knew that. He also knew that the only way to keep his hands off her before they finally decided what was to be done with their lives was to keep those hands busy. He still didn't know the whole story of the lost year between them. The year she had vanished from his life. So he waited, knowing she could come to it sooner or later. Long before Krakatoa, he hoped fervently. The fierce heat had not lessened, and a man could go mad from such things.

Hanson had spread out his tools among the phonograph parts. A screwdriver, pliers, hammer and an assortment of nuts, bolts and screws. He was all too mindful of Laura, poised at his shoulder, watching him.

"Where?" he growled.

She had seen his frown and indicated one item on the assorted pile on the table.

"Right there." She laughed.

"Ahhh." He scooped up the required bracket, smiling at her. Damn but she was a beauty. She had always been beautiful. She wore it like a queen. Or that madonna she so resembled.

He set the piece in place and reached for the screwdriver.

As he worked, he subtly stole into the heart of the great matter that stood between them. The dim lamps of the cabin were a proper setting for telling the truth at last.

"But you do remember saying good-bye to me at Batavia?" he prodded, even as he worked.

"Of course."

"What ship did you take back to Anjer?" He was being conversational, easy in his manner, so she wouldn't fly away or hide behind her womanly skirts.

"You know what ship." His question puzzled her.

"I do?" He fit a washer around a screw.

" 'Indies Cloud.' " Her tone was suddenly impatient.

" 'Indies Cloud,' yes. Was Travis expecting you?"

"I don't remember." She paused, uncertain. "Chris, why are you asking me about—"

"What did he say?" he continued blandly.

"I've just told you. I don't know."

He was persistent. "Had he heard about us?"

"Chris—it's been too long." She was being evasive and he sensed it.

He looked up from his work. She lowered her eyes.

"It's too hot," she murmured. "I'm too tired . . . it's . . . just too painful . . ."

"Sooner or later it has to be talked about."

"Not tonight, please. I was just feeling halfway at ease for the first time in a long time. Talking with Mr. Rigby, I almost felt that I was helping another person for a change."

"Let's try helping you." He had casually continued with his phonograph assemblage.

"No, thank you," she said firmly.

Hanson now stared dead level into her troubled eyes.

"At St. Margaret's, you didn't eat, couldn't sleep and refused to talk. How could they help you under those circumstances?"

"I didn't *ask* for help," she snapped.

"But you needed it," he reminded her. She couldn't look at him now. She stared around the room restlessly.

"He knew we'd been seeing one another?" Hanson asked.

"Yes." It was obviously a reluctant admission.

"Did he anticipate your asking him for a divorce?"

"I don't know."

"He didn't say whether—"

"He was abusive," she said sharply. "He said a lot of things. Mostly what he was saying was no."

"Tell me," he asked softly.

Her mind was in a turmoil. She kept staring at him, her

eyes begging for some of the mercy he had shown Harry Connerly.

"He said . . . that if I attempted to divorce him . . . I would never see my boy. He would take Peter away. Chris . . . he didn't want the marriage and he didn't want the divorce. We had a terrible fight." Memory had left some awe in her.

He waited for her to go on. When she didn't, he urged her with a questioning "And?"

"Nothing." She shook her head.

"Go on."

"That's all."

"That's all he said or—"

"That's all I remember."

He was plainly skeptical, toying with the screwdriver.

"Well, did *you* leave? Did *he?*"

"I suppose . . ." She was uneasy. ". . . he left."

"Then?"

"Then . . . nothing."

"Try," he pleaded.

"No," she answered instantly.

"What was the last—the very last thing he said?"

"I've told you!" She was showing anger now.

Hanson said flatly, "Then he would take Peter if you asked for a divorce. Then you said—what exactly?"

"Nothing," she wailed brokenly. "I mean I don't . . . I can't think."

"Well, did you say—"

"My God, Chris, stop it!"

He wouldn't stop. He couldn't.

"If you had agreed not to ask for a divorce, Peter would still be with you."

She was trying not to listen, the lovely face contorted with the grief she had been carrying locked inside.

"Wouldn't he?" Hanson said pointedly.

She got up suddenly, starting for the door. He had anticipated that. He stepped ahead of her, blocking her retreat. She whirled again, crossing to the far wall. He watched her closely.

"And you would be with Travis. So you didn't agree not to ask for a divorce."

Laura turned a face on him that held anger, frustration and internal upheaval. He had never seen so far beneath her placid exterior.

"Don't keep after me, Chris!"

"Then answer!" he rasped harshly. "What did you say to him?"

Hate was etched across her glare.

"What–did–you–say–to–Travis?" Hanson roared, emphasizing every word. The cabin rang with his ferocity. So much depended on her answer—the answer he had to hear.

"Go to hell!" she screamed at him fiercely. Tears flooded her eyes. "That's what I said! I told him he couldn't hurt me with his threats. I was going back to you with or without a divorce." She stared at Hanson for a long second, and when she spoke again, it was with a more quiet intensity. "I don't think I even realized what I was saying. He stormed through the house and then after I don't know how long, it was quiet. He had taken Peter . . . I had let him take my little boy away. My feeling for you had . . . distorted everything. It slowly began to settle in that I was never going to see my son again. I ran to the dock. The 'Adrianna' was just leaving the harbor." Tears spilled from her eyes. "I let him go, didn't I? I haven't admitted that for a *year*. Chris, I have no right to a life if Peter is dead. He would never have been on that ship if . . ." Her voice broke again. She pressed her hands to her face.

Hanson moved to her to take her in his arms. She pulled back. He did not touch her.

His face held compassion, love and understanding.

"A year ago," he murmured, "you walked off the far side of the earth. You weren't with me anymore and there was a hole in my life big enough to sail this ship through. I love you and I know that"—he touched her face with a soft finger—"inside this pretty head, you know we're feeling guilty, you and I, as long as your little boy is missing. You'll never forgive us until we find him."

Her eyes had never left his face. She seemed absorbed with some of his strength, his determination. There was great power and masculinity in Hanson. Hope almost grew in her eyes. The true closeness and love she had for Hanson had suddenly come home to her with full force, flood-tide. The only restriction, as he had said, was the vast painful concern for her son.

"And that's what we're going to do," Hanson muttered grimly. "Find him."

The heat had not lessened, but hope, the thing eternal in the human heart, had suddenly blossomed in Hanson's quarters.

The manner in which he had stated his vow made Laura

Travis certain that if anybody could locate Peter Travis, Chris Hanson could.

If Peter were truly, miraculously alive . . .

She fervently prayed that he was.

Leoncavallo Borghese and Toshi Namura had found some degree of comfort in the chain locker room where Harry Connerly had had his terrible ordeal. Toshi had unearthed a grass mat and a porcelain bowl, setting them up in a niche of the room where the shadows lay darkest. She had brought along a brightly colored cloth which she immersed in the water of the bowl and drew forth dripping wet. This she was applying to Leoncavallo's wrist as he lay back against a bulkhead. In the gloom, both young people, acutely aware of the infernal temperature, were also keenly aware of each other. Days and nights on the *Batavia Queen*, the deck strolls after dark, the tinikling dances, the long East and West talks, all of this had drawn them together.

"This place and the throat are where the blood is closest to the surface. A cool cloth here will cool the entire body, they say."

"For about one second." Leoncavallo laughed.

"Also, it helps to think of other things. I will tell you more of Japan. Of my village."

"No," he whispered ardently in the dampness of the locker room. "Just about Toshi."

He held her hand, moving closer to her. They sat in silence, digesting the precious moment of aloneness, togetherness. It was as if they were in a peaceful, though hot, bower, cut off from the rest of the ship and the rest of the world. Neither of them could have been aware of the immense, miles-wide fog slowly crawling forward over the sea, coming on like a tremendous mantle of darkness to envelop the ship. On deck, the watch were viewing the approaching monster with all the terror inherent in voyages into little-charted seas. The devils that had beset the *Batavia Queen* were mounting rapidly.

"I am only permitted to dive for a certain number of years, then a younger girl will take my place." Toshi's sweet voice was like a carol in the shadows. "I go home. To marry."

"To . . . marry?" Leoncavallo sat up at that. "Who?"

"Someone in my village." Her eyes gleamed at him in the

gloom. "You will marry someone from where you live, as your parents wish?"

"No, not exactly." His grin was rueful. "And I haven't parents. I have parent. Singular. A father."

"You are very fortunate. After my mother and father died, I was raised by English missionaries until I was fourteen, when my uncle remembered me. Fourteen is the age at which girls begin as pearl divers in my uncle's village. You are so fortunate to have a father who loves you." She saw the sarcasm on his face. "You do not think so?"

Leoncavallo's initial instinct had been to laugh. To make light of his charming but ineffectual father. But his quick grin dimmed as he saw the comparison of his own life with that of the lovely soul before him.

"I—ah, yes. Yes, I suppose so."

"It is true. I know it from the morning when he watched us dance. The second time you danced tinikling with me."

"What happened then?"

"When you are dancing tinikling, I looked up. He was watching you, your father. Because you laugh, he smiles, he is happy." She shrugged simply. "So you see, I know . . . Leoncavallo."

He was moved by her insight, by the fact that a litle Oriental girl had taken note of his relationship with Giovanni Borghese.

"Well, that's very observant," he admitted. Suddenly he was ill at ease. He changed the subject, affecting a brasher manner. "Now if this expedition is properly successful and we live through it, what will you do with all that money?"

"Nothing."

"Not anything?" He was astonished.

"I will give my share to my uncle, of course."

"Not if I have anything to say about it."

"But you will not, Leoncavallo."

"How can you be sure?" He touched her fingertips. "Listen, Toshi—"

"You are very young," she said sadly, her delicate hands in his. "Your heart reaches out easily still. You are being very kind."

He slowly drew her to him. Her piquant face curved up like a lotus flower to meet his. Their lips were a breath apart. Leoncavallo's heart soared. In the gloom, he read her soul and read it well.

"No, no," he murmured. "Not kind. Toshi . . ."

She almost surrendered. She tried once more to distract him, beckoning toward the thickening fog blanketing the entrance of the chain locker. The quiet ominous mass had moved like a thief in the night to overwhelm the decks of the ship.

"Leoncavallo, such a strange cloud. It covers—"

He was beyond caring about the weather, the heat, the fog. He surrounded her with hungry arms, trapping her in a fierce, hot kiss. His lips burned against her mouth.

Startled, Toshi Namura responded.

The fog, unheeded, claimed the *Batavia Queen* in another kind of kiss.

The kiss of death, more treacherous than any known to lovers.

At the wheelhouse windows, Hanson narrowed his gaze, trying to break the density of the all-enveloping cloud covering the ship. His vision was totally obstructed. It was difficult enough to see his hand before his face. There was a wall of mist in front of him.

"Soup!" he muttered disgustedly to Jacobs, standing by at his elbow. "Reduce speed to dead slow, take soundings until this clears."

The telegraph clanged jarringly in immediate reply. Jacobs stifled a yawn. Hanson turned his attention to the chart table. The damned pea soup hovered over the wheelhouse, creeping through the doors and windows like a tide of locusts in a plague.

At the shrouded bow, Midori, Sumi and Kiko stared helplessly like terrified children into the nothingness. There was a wash of magenta streaking the wall of fog. They could hear Mr. Jacobs shouting in the gloom though they could not see him. *"Break out the lead line!"* Baffled, Toshi's diving companions exchanged glances among themselves. The fog was so monstrous it covered the universe. It was as if there were nothing else, could be nothing else. Fearful, the girls huddled, whispering.

In the forward hold, the convicts, their zenith of displeasure reached and surpassed, stared dumbly at the bilious fog curling down into their gloomy cavern of confinement. They drew back in dread, afraid to be touched by the fog. The Dutch guard gripped his black truncheon and gazed about in superstitious awe. The sullen brutishness of his face had become a mask of fear. Fear of the unknown.

All about the ship, seamen moved, speaking in low mutters, trying to pierce the strange fog, to understand it. The shouted cries of Jacobs' detail to take soundings only added to the apprehension. The obscuring mist closed off all view and perspective. The voices sounded ghostlike and hollow in the darkness.

"Fifteen fathoms!"

Ninety feet . . . sweet mother of God . . . that was too damned low for this stretch of ocean. . . .

The fog-enveloped steamer stalked like a wraith through the blanket of mist. The muzzled sound of her two-stroke engines lent an unreal, ominous undertone to the muttering voices of the men standing along the rail, trying to pierce the towering majesty of the gloom.

Charley Adams watched the shreds of orange fog drifting through the porthole of her cabin. She frowned, her nostrils curling as the noxious bite of fumes assailed her. It smelled horrible.

"Harry, is it all right if I close this thing? It's cooler now."

"Sure, close it."

Connerly was sprawled on his bunk. He was bending his knees, flexing them experimentally, painfully. The cramps from his enforced sojourn in the hanging box-cage had not completely left him. He had been soaking his elbows and joints for hours with cold compresses. Nothing seemed to help the scorched texture of his flesh.

Charley slammed the porthole door, clamping the lugs in place. When she had done, she paced the floor of the cabin aimlessly, arms folded. There was agitation in her. As bad as Connerly felt, he was not unaware of her condition.

She was making conversation, too. Something she had never had to force before, or reach for. They had always been able to talk to each other. Connerly paused in his labors and studied her. Old Goldilocks was acting like she'd met the three bears and they had scared her plenty.

Charley wrinkled her nose.

"There's kind of a smell in the air. You notice? Like old eggs?"

"Sulfur," he said thinly. Fire and brimstone for devils like Harry Connerly.

"You want some more water or a damp cloth?"

He looked at her. Quietly he asked, "What's the matter, Charley?"

She jerked as if he had caught her in a lie. She tried a weak smile. A wisp of leftover fog touched her dress.

"I—uh—nothing. Not anything, really. The fog's kind of spooky, I guess. But . . ."

She started pacing again, anxious to talk about something else. Connerly returned to his knee exercises. He grunted with the strain. Each movement produced a spasm of discomfort.

"You did all right, Charley," he reassured her, "when Hanson had me up in that box. You did fine."

"Ah—" She showed embarrassment. "It's okay, Harry. You're the one it was hard for. Humiliating."

He got up, straightening with an effort. He intercepted her in her aimless pacing. His hands took her shoulders and turned her about easily to face him.

"Charley, somethin's pinchin' somewhere . . . this isn't how you act. One of them say something about you?"

"No." Hurriedly she blinked. "Gosh, Harry, I just felt so . . . so funny."

It was spilling out of her now. The tension, the dread, the hurts of all the days and nights with Harry Connerly. He held her close to him, recognizing her need to talk, her hope that he would listen for once. And really understand.

"They didn't *say* anything or . . . anything, but I knew what they thought you did to that girl. Gosh, Harry, what do you suppose they think of me?" The anguish in her rushed to the surface, erupting as the dam within her broke.

Connerly stepped back from her, staring. This was a revelation to him. Something he had never thought about. This bright, quick, rough-and-ready dame worried about what people thought of her! That was something. That was a new one. For a second, he doubted he had heard her right. Charley Adams?

But her face told him what he wanted to know.

Slowly, thoughtfully, he said, "I never knew it worried you."

Almost shyly, she smiled.

"Sometimes I forget and act like a girl." She brushed a long tress of golden-blond hair away from her forehead. He reached out and pushed it back gently.

"Well, watch your step. One o' these days I might bust up a good friendship and marry you."

An expression of total surprise froze her face into a mold of disbelief.

"You never even kidded about that before, Harry."

"Well, I'm kiddin' about it now so don't send out any announcements, all right?"

Her expression brightened. He bent over the washbasin

and poked a forefinger. "Damn it, Charley," he growled. "The water's warm again."

She grinned, bouncing for the door, a new life and joy in her lithe movements. "Right away, Harry."

When the door closed behind her, Connerly looked after her for a timeless moment. Then he massaged his painful right shoulder and winced.

But his eyes were full of thought.

Thoughts he had never had before.

Not ever.

Especially about women.

The dripping, rising lead lines coming up alongside the hull of the *Batavia Queen* served only to indicate the perilous position of the ship. The depth was getting shallower, the solid fog bank as impenetrable as any stone wall. The bridge could not be seen from the bow of the ship where spotters strove to pierce the darkness. Kuan entered the wheelhouse, his face grim as death. Hanson, crouched at the helm, stared earnestly ahead. He seemed to be listening, trying to catch a clue as to the position of the ship.

"Stop engines!" Hanson ordered.

Kuan marveled at the wheelhouse; it was totally fogged in and he could barely identify the two ship's officers flanking the captain. Jan was close by, identifiable only because he was closest. The unearthly fog had blotted out practically everything.

The telegraph jangled in the gloom. The ship lurched to a full stop. The silence about them packed the men in like wet cotton. Kuan felt like an object prepared for shipment to the East Indies. He heard Jacobs' voice now, speaking from Hanson's left: "It could have been thunder. There might be a storm out there somewhere."

Hanson held up a cautioning hand. Still trying to catch some sound he could operate by, he didn't answer Jacobs. It was useless. Kuan could tell. The pea soup, thicker than ever, rolled on inexorably.

Kuan sniffed the air. "Feels like a breeze coming up," he offered.

"*Shhh!*" Jacobs hissed.

The silence continued for a long measure of time in the haze-bound atmosphere of the wheelhouse. Then it became a distant, menacing rumble of noise. A bone-shaking cataract of sound, distorted by the fog so that it seemed to emanate from the very air around them. All the men tensed, ready for anything. Nothing happened. Only the great roar of noise swirling about their ears, deafening them.

Hanson flung a look toward the wheelhouse door, sensing someone there. It was Laura Travis, standing in the rippling mists, distraught, frightened. Hanson held out his arms and she rushed into them. The ghastly thunder echoed again.

"I'm terrified," she moaned. "It's all been like a series of warnings, Chris. This smoke is the most frightening of all. Is it Krakatoa again?"

Jacobs grunted. "It better not be."

Hanson flung him a sharp look before answering Laura.

"We don't know what it is."

The breeze that Kuan had noticed suddenly blew lightly over the wheelhouse interior, ruffling the scattered papers on the table. Hanson moved to one side. Laura followed him. This was the strangest happening of all. A breeze! A fresh wind! No fog ever produces a breeze—the air currents don't work that way. . . .

On the bridge, a fine wind tugged their clothing, flowed their hair. They stared hard forward, Hanson absolutely astounded by the indescribable movements of fog, wind and sky. Fleetingly, through the gauzelike, obfuscating breeze, there were patches of light and grayish streaks. The fog was thinning. Incredibly, swiftly. As if the *Batavia Queen* were running through a curtain that stretched from sea to sky. A looming gigantic shape of indefinite nature came and went, standing on the flat sea. Like something seen through a glass, darkly.

Hanson reacted instantly.

Over his shoulder, he shouted instructions to Jacobs.

"Alert the Borgheses and Mr. Rigby. Shake out the compressor crew. Have the balloon and diving equipment made ready."

Jacobs stared for one long second past Hanson's shoulder, his face twisted with shock and surprise, then, suspending his normal curiosity, he moved quickly to obey the instincts of a lifetime at sea.

Abruptly, weirdly, the strange orange fog with magenta splashes had lifted. The nothingness vanished. The sun and sea and sky sprang sharply into focus, as if they had merely been hiding and now chose this moment to reveal themselves in all their splendor and glory. Yet the far horizon was truly the earthshaking view of any man's lifetime. Hanson let out his breath slowly. He could feel Laura's fingernails digging into his palm. He could scarcely blame her for her agitation, her fright.

The towering, mountainous, malefic volcano, the one Douglas Rigby called the powder keg, stood exposed in awesome, breathtaking grandeur. Like something monolithic, pagan, splendid and terrible. Mighty Krakatoa. From its jagged, cratered cone climbed a steady stream of yellow-red smoke, the identical color and density of the peculiar orange fog.

Krakatoa spewed, bellowed and thundered. Sights and sounds older than time itself.

"Chris—" Laura Travis whispered in a stupefied voice.

"Krakatoa," he said simply.

The initial wonder dissolved into apprehensive dread and fear. Laura Travis shook like an aspen leaf in a high wind. The fog was gone but had been replaced by a stronger adversary.

The volcano known as Krakatoa dwarfed the horizon.

BOOK TWO

KRAKATOA

As the radiantly clear skies spread a contrasting panorama of beauty, Krakatoa jutted spectacularly from the sea itself. The beach, alien, dark and threatening, curled like a ribbon about his hidden base. The *Batavia Queen* riding at anchor in the murky tropical shallows had immediately and efficiently followed the dictums of Captain Chris Hanson, as if there were no time to lose. Mighty Krakatoa was silent, only the distant plumage of the smoke column rising from his cone, but there was no telling when he would awaken again and spew the area with molten lava and destruction. Ship's bells tolled in the stillness. Against its message, the crew and all hands and specialists and experts made ready. There was a feverish excitement among the souls on board. With the lifting of the fog and the explanation of the phenomena of the bursting lights, banshee sounds and the strange mist itself, all spirits had lifted to a keen pitch. The treasure hunt was on and even the helplessly imprisoned human cargo of convicts in the hold could sense the tumult of endeavor and activity going on above their heads.

The Borghese balloon, its huge orange skin inflated and its white canopy fluttering in a stout breeze, was held fast on the beach, ready for the ascent. A detail of the ship's crew, rugged seamen to whom this device was a strange toy, stood at the ready, holding fast to the four heavy mooring ropes. Each of these lines was lashed to a heavy sandbag which held the balloon captive. In the wicker basket beneath the giant observation contraption, Giovanni and Leoncavallo Borghese made final adjustments, checking the manually operated propellor and rudder. Leoncavallo, his youthfully vital face grinning, was amused with the standby crew's incredulity and amazement. The goggle-eyed sailors were something to see. Leoncavallo could not resist a jibe at his father's expense.

"A very small audience for you, Poppa."

Giovanni looked at him sharply, then smiled. His son's remark had pointedness but was also very apt.

"Well, we suggest insanity to them. We also suffer." He arched his eyebrows. "And the pay is better than carnivals."

"We hope."

"One always hopes, Leoncavallo." The older man's tone was meaningful. He placed his hand on his son's shoulder. Leoncavallo permitted the gesture, but only for a moment. He turned away on the pretense of seeing to a rope fastening. Borghese absorbed the mild rebuff with a philosophical shrug. Then the business at hand engulfed him. The same high sense of adventure which had made him an aeronaut in the very first place. The fine smell of the air, the dizzying expanse of the blue sky, the utter wonder of space and room to breathe, far from the dusky, musky wine cellars of his younger days when his naked feet had endlessly crushed a millennia of purple grapes.

He gestured grandly at the waiting crewmen on the ground. "Gentlemen," he said with great cheer, spreading his hands to show it was time. On the signal, the lashing ropes were unwound, the mooring posts stood naked and there came that exciting first quick jolt of freedom. Leoncavallo began to hum under his breath. Borghese bowed to the ground crew. Soon the balloon lifted, fluttering upward like a bright orange bird. *The Flying Borgheses* had taken to the air again.

The faces of the ground crew receded. The balloon soared.

In less than an instant, it was airborne, swaying, tipping, swinging in a wide arc high above the beach and earth and sea, going on a swift, guided tangent toward the mighty awesome environs of Krakatoa. The rocky face of the volcano shone starkly on the horizon.

Holding firm on the rudder bar, Giovanni Borghese bore down rapidly on Krakatoa.

On the bridge of the *Batavia Queen*, Hanson surveyed the ascent of the balloon through a pair of worn leather binoculars. As a seaman, the navigation of all devices was of paramount interest to him, despite his solid interest in the purposes of the Borgheses' reconnaissance flight. Once the balloon was aloft, however, he turned his attention to the forward deck.

He saw the diving girl, Toshi. She was hugging the port rail, as though hanging on for life, watching the tiny ball of gas and skin rising higher and higher in the sky. A fresh movement of the wind was spiraling the balloon. Hanson understood Toshi's concern. He had not been blind to the love affair going on under everyone's nose. It was all too apparent that Borghese's boy and the Japanese diver had reached the point of love. Hanson shook his head bitterly. A wonderful commodity, yet it reminded him all too harshly of how his own feeling for Laura Travis had caused her to lose her little boy.

Mildly troubled, he pushed the thought from his mind. He had no time for guilt. He must begin preparations for the sea portion of the search for Mr. Travis' precious pearls.

At his commands and with Douglas Rigby's necessary guidance, the diving bell device was resting on the forward hatch. The slab-sided steel object gleamed like a curiously large coffin in the hazy sunlight. The attachments had been completed; hawser cables rigged to a heavy overhead boom. The bell was ready to be swung over the side to be lowered into the sea. Douglas Rigby, his youthful face expectant and prepared, was easing himself into the bleak, metallic interior of the thing. For once, the young scientist had been sensible. He had forsaken his habitual costume of white tropical ducks for a heavy woolen sweater and a pair of seaman's trousers. A sock cap held down his thatch of yellow hair. The steel door closed shut behind him. The steam winch let out a blast of vapor as the machinery clanked alive. *Butterfly III* took to the air, swinging up on high, halting, the boom moving like a man's arm, straight out, poising the bell above the water. The winch operator jerked a handle and *Butterfly III* disappeared slowly, gently, into the depths. The green waters of the bay closed over her steel hull.

Laura Travis watched the operation from the quarterdeck. On the north, she could see the Borghese balloon still soaring, gaining altitude. Borghese had not activated the propellor as yet. The balloon seemed outlined against the standing rigging of the ship, but it was only an illusion.

Still, it served to worry Hanson. He frowned upward, murmuring to Jacobs who had drawn closer to his side as was his custom.

"They're drifting off-course."

"Never get me up in one of those things," Jacobs said.

Midships, Harry Connerly was being outfitted in his heavy

diving suit with the help of two stout sailors. The rubber uniform made Connerly's normally big body bulk larger. Only the globular steel helmet remained to be circled around Connerly's head and screwed down to the metal collar of the suit. Connerly had paused to watch the erratically dodging balloon in the sky. Charley Adams, her face hiding her fears for Harry, had her hand on his shoulder.

"They'll be all right, Harry," she said. "Poppa Borghese knows his stuff."

"Yeah," Harry Connerly grunted.

Leoncavallo was wrestling with the propellor. His father, bland face betraying a slight lack of calm, assisted him. Both men were spurred on in their efforts by a disquieting explosion from nearby Krakatoa. A modest blast of sulfurous smoke funneled impressively from the top of the volcano. Borghese stepped back as Leoncavallo spun the propellor successfully, working the hand levers expertly. The balloon righted itself, correcting the position as Borghese had wanted. The buoyant ball rose dizzily, clearing the danger, swaying from side to side, stretching its arms in the air. Borghese looked down, conscious of a faint veil of perspiration on his forehead.

The view was incredibly beautiful—and ugly.

He could see the shoals, reefs and depths surrounding the island in a never-ending circle of terror. Krakatoa loomed up out of the wide sea like a stunning monster from the depths. The floor of the ocean was clearly visible even from this height. Shells, coral heads and curious objects that Borghese did not know gleamed like diamonds on display in a store window in Firenze. The colors were preposterously beautiful and strange: silvery lights, pure greens, dark blues, splashes of crimson—almost every color of the rainbow. Borghese strained his eyes as the balloon leveled on its course.

Yet there was nothing resembling a wrecked ship beneath the sea. No sign of the *Adrianna*.

Still, there was hope. The search had just begun, and after all, the balloon was now performing beautifully. On command. And Leoncavallo's hand was sure and experienced on the rudder.

Underwater, in the amazing world of the sea, Douglas

Rigby was enjoying that highly special position of seeming to be the only human being in the universe. The plate-glass observation window of *Butterfly III* had opened up a frontier of amazement, wonder and great truth. As cramped and confined as the interior of the bell was, Rigby felt no discomfort. There was far too much to see, to know, to learn, to understand, for mere inconveniences to disturb him. The sensation of uniqueness and oneness was overpowering.

The kingdom of the sea was another terrestrial, another land. A world without end. With a million and one delights and marvels for the scientific mind.

Through the glass, he drank his fill.

The sea beyond was a green, jungle-like terrain, stretching endlessly before him. Low-lying coral formations, their perforated walls looking formidable, nonetheless lay shimmeringly beautiful. Large sea fans swept by the corner of his eyes. Rigby, his breath dry and suspended, couldn't take his gaze off the ever-changing, ever-fantastic world around him. It was an odyssey of science, something to talk about and remember for the rest of one's life.

Butterfly III moved through the depths. The cosmos of sea and underwater creatures accompanied the bell. Rigby glowed with knowledge and enthusiasm. His busy fingers made notations on the chart board clamped to his knee. Hanson would want to know a lot, too. He knew that the captain was following his progress on one of the many charts in the wheelhouse. Rigby had never known a more thorough-going man. Absolutely rules and regulations in all departments. Quite like a red-tape Englishman, really. Rigby smiled at the thought.

Lost in the charm of his fresh new environment, Rigby was suddenly jarred back to reality. A huge coral formation, jagged, sharp and cruel, showed directly ahead, filling the glass window before him. A formidable, dangerous mass. The crusted obstacle loomed with terrifying speed.

Rigby grabbed the speaking tube. "Take me up! Four or five fathoms. Quickly!"

The giant coral structure was approaching with the speed of a motor lorry now. Rigby held his breath, waiting. He stared at the speaking tube and bit his lip. Seconds stretched into an agonizing space of time. At last, seemingly none too soon, the bell lurched and jerked upward, rising to clear the coral formation as the sea floor fell away beneath the steel bottom of *Butterfly III*. Rigby expelled his relief in a bursting gust of air.

He had gauged the height of the coral formation accurately.

He settled down again, once more occupying himself with the weird underwater world beyond his prison of steel and glass. The bell moved forward again, inching now through the fantasy of marine life. The colors, the sights, the silence, were a tremendous amalgam of continual delight.

And danger.

Father should see his son's "chamber pot" now. . . .

Hanson had overseen the preparations of Toshi and her diving girls. A lifeboat had been made ready, hanging from its davits a few feet above the water line. At the side of the hatch, the girls readied themselves for their descent into the sea. On the hatch cover lay the implements of their craft. Short knives attached to leather thongs to be worn about the waist. Improvised goggles with lenses of mica and frames of shell and cloth. The diving costume itself would be the short, tight sarong, closely wrapped about the slender bodies. Hanson checked the weather. The sky was still bright with haze. Krakatoa rumbled in the distance. The Borghese balloon looked like a strange bird in flight. No telling what was up with the diving bell. Except for a few narrow squeaks, Rigby had said little over the speaking tube. Hanson, to keep his nerves under control, had supervised the cleaning down of the greasy, rusty winch. It had been steam-cleaned so that its levers and gears were freed of rust and sludge. A fouled line had killed more men than Hanson cared to remember. In or out of diving bell contraptions.

Connerly was still waiting in his heavy diving suit, with the golden-haired Charley Adams keeping him company. She couldn't seem to take her eyes off the Borghese balloon. It was as if she were eternally fascinated with the thought that two human beings could risk their lives in such a flimsy thing. Hanson well understood her feelings. He much preferred the sturdy decks of a ship beneath his feet.

Laura Travis, too, was positioned at the railing, her head inclined toward the sky. Hanson tried not to think about her. Or her boy, Peter. There was far too much to be done if all of them were to get out of this rich—and alive. Postmortems and regrets or rejoicing would have to come later.

So much depended on those three essentials of success: daring, skill and luck.

The Borgheses were staring down into the sea from the wicker sides of their gondola basket. Giovanni Borghese was particularly intent on something far below. Leoncavallo came to his side, adding his own eyes to the investigation of the specific spot under the surface. Excitedly, the elder Borghese was focusing his binoculars with great deliberation.

The twin lens had picked up something.

Below the level of the sea, a rocky slope, its peak flattened to form a shelflike plateau, perhaps thirty feet or more beneath the surface, dropped off into the deeper water. It was this location which had drawn Borghese's interest.

He roved with the glasses, picking up the shelf of rock and carefully, slowly, extended his inspection. The glasses hovered for a long instant. Vague, shadowy outlines of something caused Borghese to adjust the lenses. He murmured a prayer with a sharp intake of breath. The jagged, twisted forms were taking shape.

He was no seaman, knew nothing of the ocean, but he was certain that he was seeing the scattered bits and pieces of the flotsam of a wrecked ship. The *Adrianna*. Wordlessly, he passed the glasses to Leoncavallo. The young man lowered his head. In a long moment, he straightened, happiness shining from his handsome face. Borghese nodded. Leoncavallo whooped.

"That looks like it!"

"You agree?"

"Yes, of course. What do you think?"

"We have found it." Borghese smiled. He reached up to yank on the hydrogen release valve which would make them stationary a bit longer. "Shoot the Very pistol, Leoncavallo."

There was a flare gun fixed to the side of the basket. The younger man scooped the pistol, pointed it skyward, away from the balloon, and fired. The rocket cartridge left a trail of smoke before it burst into a fiery flare that splattered the sky with light and sound.

"How deep do you think it is?" Leoncavallo asked.

"We should put a marker there." There was high excitement in his father now.

Leoncavallo's head jerked as the balloon shifted course violently. "We're going to the east too far. Quickly, Poppa."

Borghese uncovered an orange marker, dumping it hastily over the side. Leoncavallo was right; the bag had moved dangerously to the east—in the direction of Krakatoa.

As the star shell exploded, the decks of the *Batavia Queen* erupted with a deeply felt emotion of excited joy. Hanson dashed into the wheelhouse, barking instructions.

"Come to three ten and hold it."

"Three ten," the helmsman echoed.

The railings were crowded with seamen. Babbling, pointing, indicating the orange balloon and the raining shreds of flare-light coming down on the waters. The vessel swung about slowly as the helmsman pulled hard on the wheel. The mighty face of Krakatoa now stood directly before the prow of the *Batavia Queen*. The helmsman swallowed nervously, brushing a sleeve against his cheek. Krakatoa towered, spumes of yellow-red smoke shooting from his jagged peak. Again, that deep, foreboding rumble of sound. The giant was stirring restlessly, as if angry with these intruders in his midst.

Laura Travis smiled slowly from the depths of the wheelhouse windows. Harry Connerly and Charley Adams matched pleased expressions. The bursting shell might have been the starting signal of a whole new life of respectability for them.

Under Hanson's skillful calculations, the ship plowed smoothly toward the colored marker afloat on the ocean. It was a bright orange dot on the waters almost directly below the hovering balloon, some one hundred feet overhead.

But the balloon was behaving erratically, jerking and bucking like a pennant in a high wind. The gondola basket was spilling, side-slipping dangerously. Hanson repressed a curse of alarm.

The propellor had broken.

Suddenly, its windmilling, gyrating arc had ceased. A snapped blade dangled. Leoncavallo stared up at it in horror.

"Poppa, the propellor! The pin probably fell out!"

Borghese, his face ashen, leaped to repair the damage. The balloon, without power, was rising out of control, heading nearly full-tilt for the summit of the volcano. The rails of the *Batavia Queen*, with Hanson at the fore, surrounded by baffled, frightened crewmen and expedition members, bore horrified witness. Connerly, on the side of the wooden platform which would lower him into the sea, heavily suited, took his eyes off the cable leading to the aft boom and followed the mad flight of the balloon. His hard fingers dug into Charley Adams' arm. She cried out in pain but he didn't hear her.

Lester Danzig, his thin face wary, had eyes only for the deck hatch and the layout of the convicts' prison. From behind the back of the Dutch guard, Danzig's slitted eyes held a meaning all their own. He scarcely paid a glance to the hopelessly drifting balloon of the Borgheses. He had other fish to fry.

The frantically working father and son team of daring aeronauts was deeply in trouble. The errant balloon had left the sea and passed over the sandy beach, and the rocky pattern of outcropping was clearly visible beneath the basket. The base of Krakatoa itself. Narrow canyons, sharp spines of rock protruding from precipitous slopes, a convoluted channel of disaster, walled and deadly, leading directly toward the climbing summit of the volcano. Wind whistled through the guy wires of the balloon. Borghese panted, tearing at the propellor desperately. Leoncavallo, in the clutch of terror, still tried to help. The balloon skirted along the canyon tunnel, skipping, missing calamity by inches until the harsh wind swept it above the canyon level. Drawn higher, helpless, the orange ball bobbed toward the steep slope of Krakatoa's peak.

Borghese cut loose two of the weighted sandbags, striving despairingly for more lift. Leoncavallo continued to struggle with the propellor. Relentlessly, the balloon was drawn toward the steaming mouth of the volcano.

On the bridge of his ship, Hanson, a telescope raised to his eye, followed the frightening flight of the Borgheses. They were doomed.

The gondola was bucketing. He could see Borghese and his son slashing at the weight bags which bordered the wicker basket, trying to gain altitude, to pull away from the volcano's crater. Smoke and vapor enveloped them as Krakatoa's hot breath fanned out.

The balloon reached the lip of the crater. It lost altitude and slowly, irrevocably fell downward into the yawning abyss.

Transfixed, all the hearts aboard the *Batavia Queen* watched the catastrophe unfold. The balloon descended past the volcano's rim into the grumbling, crackly, fiery maw. As it did so, the last of the weight sacks was cut loose, falling free. Hanson lowered the telescope, not wanting to look anymore.

Lava blasted, boiled and bubbled.

The Borgheses were falling to their fate, the bleak lava sides of the crater flashing past them in a dizzying burst of light and sound. The boiling lava surged, flowed, erupted. The crust flared open convulsively on the ridge. Bursts of fiery explosions, the crackle of boiling rock, made Borghese maniacal in his endeavors to save their lives. Frantically, he detached the heavy propellor mountings, dropping it over the side. The mechanism fell away toward the lava crust below. A white-hot shower of sparks flashed upward as the mass disappeared into the crust. A rapid series of explosions like chain lightning ripped the boiling magma below. Yellow, orange and red flames flared, geysering skyward. With a cataclysmic roar, a great detonation flung a column of fire and smoke. The Borgheses closed their eyes and prayed, the infernal heat already blistering their flesh, burning out their lungs.

For a moment, their faces were etched in phosphorescent whiteness. They stared down into their living death. Horrified, hypnotized into frozen statues.

The world had gone insane. It was unbelievable. Fantastic. A great mockery from the gods.

The massive explosion was shooting the balloon upward, flinging it like a child's discarded toy away from the scalding cone of the crater. Rocketing it free and aloft, spewing it out into the sky. Blasting the orange ball of gas into the precious fresh air. Into the liberating heavens.

But the balloon was afire. There was not time to talk about the miracle of life. A corner of the wicker basket was blazing with greedy zest. A colorful canopy, trailing smoke from the gondola, dropped slowly toward the sea.

The flames were spreading. The Borgheses, drained of energy and nerves, beat at the fire with their jackets. The father, quick to judge their height from the water, seized the valve release cords, dumping some more hydrogen. The balloon quickened its descent. To the stunned onlookers aboard the *Batavia Queen*, the flaming bag looked like a meteor trailing fire and smoke. They, too, were still incapable of assessing the miraculous escape from a volcanic death.

"Get the boat to them!" Hanson ordered Jacobs.

The blazing balloon, leaving behind a plume of smoke, passed over the ship's mast, framing its fall. The flames had forced both Borgheses to one corner of the sharply tilted basket. The flaming invention described a gradual burning parabola down to the waters.

Long before the lifeboat had been hastily dropped over the side and rowed out to the rescue of the Borgheses, the balloon had exploded in a yellow ball of fire.

But not before Giovanni and Leoncavallo Borghese had plunged headlong into the sea when the burning bag was but inches from the surface of the water.

On the crowded, wondering deck, Toshi Namura closed her eyes and thanked her gods silently for the safe deliverance of the young man she truly loved.

Douglas Rigby had made a discovery, oblivious of the great drama being played in the light of day above him. The port window of the bell had shown him a long and grotesque slope undulating with exotic vegetation. A low-lying shelf of rock, a plateau of terrain, shimmered with a strange object that he could barely make out through the murky depths.

"About ten degrees to port," his voice crackled over the speaking tube, poorly disguising his elation. "Easy . . . easy . . ." The winch above moved the bell slowly. Rigby jammed his face to the observation port. His eyes narrowed. His heart skipped wildly in his chest. A great flood of blood washed through him. The moment of discovery. A moment unlike any other in the scientific life.

Looming ahead of him on the rock shelf lay a battered ship—jaggedly truncated, but a ship all the same. There was no mistaking the outline of her, the ghostly flotsam of a wreck. It was like a mirage, viewed underwater.

"There!" Rigby blurted into the tube. "About six degrees to port."

On deck, a seaman named Sullivan, in contact with Rigby, responded to the directions, adjusting the winch cable accordingly.

"About three hundred yards . . ." Rigby instructed. Sullivan, listening at the tube, adjusted the desired distance. The winch creaked in protest.

After a long pause, Rigby's voice burst excitedly over the tube. "It's—it's the wreck, all right!" Sullivan held the mechanism, waiting. The chattering tones of Rigby came back. "Let me straight down now. But slowly." Sullivan obeyed. The cable played out farther.

Rigby's bell lowered down beyond the slope of rock, past the flora and fauna of the deep. An inquisitive school of fish made darting, rapid circles away from the descending bell. Infinitesimal in the enormity of the deep, the bell dove downward. Dropping into a maze of spiny sharp coral. Rigby peered into the next world, his enthusiasm undiminished. The grim remnants of the wreck of the *Adrianna* showed starkly against the backdrop of rock.

Suddenly, frighteningly, the bell lurched, banging onto an outcropping of coral. The cable had caught on something. Rigby felt a shudder course through him. But he didn't panic. He spoke as casually as he was able to into the tube to Sullivan. The bell had stopped moving altogether.

"Stop lowering. I seem to be hung up."

There was a grinding, sawing sound, echoing hollowly and insistently against the steel sides of the bell.

Rigby waited, wondering what to do next.
Wondering what could be done.

Harry Connerly was ready for the steel helmet and weighted shoes now. But he was taking a careful amount of time studying the depth gauge attached to the winch. The cable was unwinding slowly on the spool. The hand on the gauge fell to ninety feet and then one hundred. And still didn't quite stop. Charley Adams touched his arm, sharing whatever perturbation she was sure he felt. Connerly shrugged her off, continuing to watch the falling indicator hand. One hundred and ten, one hundred and twenty . . .

He turned and ambled aft, the heavy rubber suit slowing his usually deft stride. Charley trailed after him. Connerly scarcely glanced up at the bridge where Hanson was coordinating the search operation. Now that the Borgheses had located the wreck, the proceedings were moving right along. Lester Danzig was lounging at the rail near Hanson, his slit eyes missing nothing. Beyond his back, Krakatoa emitted a persistent, vibrating roar.

Danzig eyed Hanson conversationally.

"Ever see a diver spend so much time lookin' at a depth gauge?"

Hanson didn't answer him, motioning to some of the crew below to assist Sullivan at the winch machine. Danzig sidled in closer, confidentially.

"Connerly important in this go-round?" he asked easily.

Hanson wiped a hand against his spade beard.

"Connerly's the only man who can bring up the safe. No safe. No pearls."

"Then you're playing out a misdeal, Cap. Your diver lied to you."

Hanson turned to stare at him slowly. Searchingly. Danzig smiled, tapping himself knowingly, meaningfully, on the chest.

"Lungs. Shot."

Hanson's eyes narrowed. "Is that ship talk, Lester?"

"That is Grade A absolute fact. That business with the Japanese girl in the chain locker. Remember that? Laudanum. You're gonna have to put on a suit yourself."

Hanson didn't answer. He spun on his heel sharply and left Danzig to smile contentedly as he rocked his head back against his folded hands. He could tell, all right. Hanson was angry.

On the aft deck, Harry Connerly rigged diver's equipment to a thick belt of canvas webbing. This would hold his wire cutters, hacksaws, pliers and screwdriver. All the small metal-working, woodworking tools he might need. Charley was hovering nearby, as if afraid to let him out of her sight. He was acting so funny. Usually he would jump right into his suit and go on down, but if she didn't know him any better, she would swear he was stalling. As if he were *afraid* to go down. . . .

Hanson came forward with Jacobs and a couple of the other seamen. Hanson stopped in front of the diver's locker. There was another suit hanging there, looking like a giant, inflated, kid's balloon. Hanson was taking off his jacket and Jacobs and the two seamen were lifting the rubber suit to help him into it.

When Harry Connerly looked up and saw what was going on, the expression on his face hardened into a snarl. Hanson said nothing and continued dressing.

"What the hell d'you think you're doing?"

"Even you should be able to figure that out," Hanson said coldly, suiting up methodically.

"I signed on this rust bucket as the diver," Connerly growled. "I haven't signed off yet."

"Your lungs are gone and you use laudanum, right?"

Connerly glared at him, holding back the fury in his face.

"I'm still the only diver you've got."

Hanson's fine eyes drilled back at him, the strong sensitive face angry and tough.

"You nailed me for more money because you have a fat reputation and because I was stuck for a diver. Now you can't deliver. I don't need you."

"I can get down there and back," Connerly shouted. "What happens to me afterward is my concern."

Hanson wasn't talking to him anymore. Not even acknowledging his presence. He turned to Jacobs, his head ready for the steel helmet.

"Take over while I'm below. When Rigby signals he's in position, I'll go down and—"

Sullivan, the winchman, had burst upon them, his face sweated and strained. When he saw Hanson, the words torrented out of him like water.

"The diving bell is jammed in the coral! His air hose is cut!"

There was the briefest moment of shock at yet another of the tragedies that touch all those who trust their lives to the fickle mercies of the sea. Hanson gestured the seamen to continue dressing him. He wasn't looking at Harry Connerly. Unseen, the burly diver rushed to strap on his own equipment. The deck was in an uproar.

"Hold our position," Hanson snapped to Jacobs. "Keep some slack on the cable." He looked about. *"Toshi!"* he called.

They had anticipated him, already speeding aft toward the stern. Toshi waved, her bright face holding a tight smile. The rest of the girls, like so many tiny children, sped smoothly toward their appointed task, diving gracefully from the high stern of the vessel. Hanson walked to the diver's platform, the wooden lift which would lower him into the sea. He picked up a crowbar. Men were standing by the compressor; other crewmen waited to fit the steel helmet over his head. Hanson saw two helmets and both his brows beetled. Harry Connerly was waiting on the platform, ready to go except for the helmet which is always the last adjustment to be made. For a brief moment, the men's eyes met.

"What d'you say, Hanson?" Connerly asked quietly.

"Get it on."

Even as the crewmen rapidly slammed the globular headpiece over Connerly's head, Hanson could see the wide, grateful smile on the diver's red face. Charley Adams was smiling, too.

He could well understand what it was like to give a man a chance to live again.

Meanwhile, there was Rigby to consider.

If the young idiot's air hose was really cut, he was truly in a bad way.

It was true.

Slowly, steadily descending, the diving bell squeezed through a grotesquely huge outcropping of coral. A shift in the downward plunge had brought the cable into fatal contact with a jagged finger of razor-sharp coral. Rasping along the line, this obstacle had sliced through the air hose. The bell rocked, swinging dizzily, and then the cable lodged securely between cruel shards of coral. The air hose writhed free, bubbling air.

Rigby was hurled about in his tiny cubicle like a rubber ball, smashing from one bulkhead to the other. With superhuman effort, he turned off the air hose valve which had begun to gush water like a punctured dike. Rigby looked about wildly, panic overwhelming him. The sea shimmered beyond the port window. Deadly, all mighty. There was nothing he could do. He was trapped. In a coffin of steel of his own design and making. Father's "chamber pot" had done for him at last. . . .

The continuous water leak from the air valve made a sucking, gurgling sound that was like nothing he had ever heard. Perhaps that was because it might be the very last sound he would ever hear in this life.

He was not aware of Toshi and her diving girls, iron weights attached to lines to sink them, swirling in the green waters far above him. Nor could he know that Hanson and Connerly, stepping off the submerged wooden platform, were lowering themselves, puppet-like, deeper and deeper into the depths. Toshi and her girls had released their iron weights to glide like fish, hovering in the murky underwater world, looking for the diving bell.

Toshi saw the bell first. The cable slanted into a forest of coral. The dull red sides of the contraption shone feebly within the shadows of the reef. Toshi pedaled swiftly downward, her dark hair flowing.

On deck, the divers' lines were being paid out by the nervous, restless crewmen lowering Hanson and Connerly farther into the coral world just above the sphere. When the weighted shoes touched the sandy floor of the ocean, the divers tugged their safety lines before picking their way carefully across the treacherous coral to the bell itself.

Lester Danzig, taking advantage of the enterprise occupying the crew of the ship, ducked carefully into a companionway which would bring him via a circuitous, unobserved route to Hanson's private quarters. The brown door marked CAPTAIN had been on his mind for days.

A glance to the left, to the right, and Danzig slipped into the pleasantly dim cabin unnoticed. Memory served. In Hanson's desk, a careful rifling of three drawers brought him what he was after. A .38-caliber revolver, dark and ugly-looking. He checked the cylinders briefly, satisfied it was loaded. With a thin smile, he tucked it carefully beneath his grimy convict's shirt. Making as little noise as possible with his clanking leg irons, he slipped quietly from Hanson's cabin.

The time had come for firm hands to change the direction and fortune of the *Batavia Queen*.

And Lester Danzig was just the boy for the job.

The busy crew paid him no heed as he worked his slow passage toward the canvas-covered hatch that housed the thirty convicts. The Dutch guard was smoking a hand-rolled cigarette.

Now the crew was lowering work lines into the sea— strong cables with pry bars, metal-cutting shears, metal saws and other heavy tools attached. An acetylene torch, lighted and flaming brightly, hung on its heavy rubber tubing, bubbling as it entered the water. Connerly and Hanson would need these if Rigby was in the dilemma he seemed to be.

Down in the murky ocean, the two deep-sea divers studied the obstacles confronting them. The heavy cable that had lowered the bell was badly jammed. Connerly tugged futilely at the line. It would not budge. Hanson walked slowly about the bell, examining the extent of the snarl. Mere strength alone would not release the cable. That was obvious.

Rigby, his face turning crimson, followed their slow-motion movements from his prison. The plate-glass observatory was a look into one's own demise. He could see Hanson and Connerly prying at the encrusted coral with their wrecking bars. The pitched steel cable did not yield. Rigby's eyes swung to the leaking, gurgling air hose. His breath came hard. A sense of the world closing in on him, the lights and the colors changing, convinced him that he was losing consciousness rapidly. He tried to hang on, not really knowing how to when one had little air to breathe. The air that was left in the bell when the hose had sliced in half was now almost entirely dissipated.

Swirling above the bell, Toshi and her diving group, like mermaids out of a fantasy, kept Hanson's and Connerly's diving lines clear of the jagged coral outcroppings.

In anxious, persistent minutes, the two men had broken away the last of the encrustation. Rigby, his face showing the torture of gradual asphyxiation, pressed his head against the plate-glass window of this tomb. The water level within the bell had begun to rise, reaching the lean hips of his body.

Suddenly the diving bell was freed. With a rush of water, it dropped away, clear of the reef. The movement of the line traveled clear and true to the deck crew on board the ship. With great speed, the winch was started up again. There was pressure on the cable. Slowly, Rigby's proud capsule was lifted inexorably from the floor of the ocean.

The Japanese divers, their task accomplished, swam with it, pawing briskly, stroking easily for the surface. Hanson and Connerly turned away, directing their attention toward the coral formation and the hidden prize secreted in its shadows. The *Adrianna*. The ghostly, grim outline of a wreck that meant a fortune in pearls to the finders.

The hulk, serene and rust-ridden, lay directly below them. The two men stalked the wreck, looking like strange underwater denizens as they clumped forward. Their long lifelines followed them, trailing them like ropes.

The Dutch guard on the convicts' hold had treated himself to a mug of coffee as he followed the rescue operations of Hanson's crew. He did not see Lester Danzig approaching from his rear. The guard was a trifle nervous; all of this sea business was new to him. He had left his rubber truncheon on the deck beside his feet. Danzig swept it up, moving like a ferret, smashing the heavy club down on the guard's defenseless skull. He fell heavily, never knowing what had hit him. Danzig yanked the key ring from his belt, not waiting to see whether the man was dead or alive.

When the hatch cover opened above them, the convicts clustered miserably in the darkness, blinking at the bright sunlight. They recoiled, startled. And then Danzig dropped the ring of keys among them. No explanation or stories were needed. They knew Danzig. The convict nearest the dropped key ring scooped it up with a feverish whimper of joy. There was a mad scramble in his direction. The hold vibrated with mingled elation and excitement.

The sun beat down, like the coming of the Lord. A halo of triumph, freedom and life itself.

Danzig had plotted his mutiny well.

The next move was even better: a sharing of the wealth with others to do the dirty work. The hard part. All one had to do was be smarter and foxier and know when to jump in.

The time had come.

Taking over the crew while Hanson was below would be like taking candy from babies.

Without Hanson, the *Batavia Queen* was like a ship without a rudder.

Through his face-plate, Connerly watched Hanson. He had taken hold of the descending acetylene torch. Both men had pulled themselves cautiously aboard the crumbled wreck of the *Adrianna*. You had to be careful with wrecks. A long time under the sea does strange things to wood and metal. Treachery was the long suit of the sea. With this knowledge in mind, Hanson and Connerly walked gingerly through the jagged, destroyed superstructure of the sunken vessel. Hanson was searching for the master's cabin. Connerly realized that. The wreck was firm beneath their weighted shoes, except for a slight tremor as disintegrating fragments broke loose from the main and floated off, spiraling like a new breed of fish in the depths.

There was a door along the starboard rail. With extreme care, Hanson edged through it. Connerly followed, mindful of his hose line. The dimly lit cabin lay bathed in a shimmering blue-green light. In the gloom, Hanson could make out a large ship's safe, standing like a squat emperor before a bulkhead. He spied the bolts and the signs of welding. Connerly hovered alongside of him, pointing one heavy glove. Hanson nodded, bringing the acetylene torch into play. Its hissing, fusing glare cast awesome, frightening shadows in the dead cabin of a dead ship.

The torch, placed against the upper left section of the door edge of the safe, hit home. Sparks flew. Connerly assisted, holding the torch steady as Hanson wielded it. Within minutes, the torch was cutting through the hard layer of steel binding that locked the safe to the bulkhead.

Connerly felt his face steaming up behind the face-plate. He licked his dry lips, trying to keep his head clear. The agony in his lungs, ever present, was even more tangible down here where it counted. In the deeps. He put his teeth together and held on. He wasn't going to turn the yellow card, not in front of Hanson. He owed the man that much.

Hanson crouched behind the acetylene torch, helmeted and weird, the glare of the burning tool holding fast to its task. Connerly waited, not daring to breathe too deeply. It hurt like hell every time he did.

Slowly, tiring noticeably now, Connerly began to slump within the confines of his rubber suit.

The lungs, dammit.

It was always the lungs.

The diving bell lifted from the water, sloshing, dripping, and the winch cable swung it high above deck. When it came down with a slight thump and the hatch handle was pulled back, Douglas Rigby fell into the waiting arms of his saviors. Hands reached out to help him. Dirty, grimy hands. Despite his acute lack of oxygen and his blur of vision, Rigby could sense something wasn't quite right. Through a haze, he saw convict uniforms, the man Danzig waving a black pistol, the mute sullen faces of the members of Hanson's crew. The golden-haired Miss Adams, the Borgheses, Mrs. Travis—all of them, standing about as though dazed.

Suffocated, gasping for breath, Rigby tried to make some sense out of what he was seeing. It was useless. His aching chest and pounding head made that impossible. All he was really conscious of, and eternally grateful for, was that he was alive and not dead. *Butterfly III* had not let him down.

He closed his eyes and smiled happily.

Down below, Hanson had accomplished his purpose. The heavy, cumbersome safe was freed from the bulkhead wall. He busied himself securing the heavy cables about it. Meanwhile, he was well aware of Connerly's fatigue. The big man was drooping. He could tell by the slowness of each gesture as Connerly assisted him. They had better get topside as soon as possible. The wreck was beginning to lurch a bit, settling with the addition of their weight on its dead decks. The removal of the safe made a difference, too.

Hanson guided the safe through the door, tugging the cable for firmness. Connerly was unable to help now. Grimly, Hanson wrestled the safe to a position for lifting to the surface. He gave the cable line a rough tug. Then he jerked his own lifeline before going to Connerly's side. He tugged the big man's line also and wrapped his rubber arms firmly around Connerly's waist. Through the plate-glass mask, he could see that Connerly's eyes were closed. The professional diver's tongue was lolling. It might be too late already.

It seemed an eternity before there was an answering tug on the lines. Hanson's heart soared. The squat square safe was lifting above him, slowly gaining height. Then his own line and Connerly's moved. Slowly, all three heavy, weighted figures rose from the shrouded, forgotten decks of the *Adrianna*, a foaming wake of tiny bubbles following after.

The mysterious dark green world of the underwater cosmos was left behind. The ascent was on in earnest. Hanson could begin to see the reflections of sunlight shimmering above him. He even imagined he could hear the far-off thunder of Krakatoa, stirring once more.

And there was Toshi and her girls, spiraling upward, their trim, lovely figures guiding the lifelines, keeping them clear of all hazards.

Whatever happened, if Connerly wasn't dead, the salvage operation had been a success.

He wasn't worried about Douglas Rigby. Scientists were hard to kill. Especially very young, very enthusiastic ones. They could take a great deal of punishment. More than even he had a right to demand.

In this frame of mind, Hanson rose to the surface of the

bay to find the safe, his crew and his passengers in the not so tender hands of one Lester Danzig.

A Danzig who had a gun.

A Danzig who meant never to be in chains again.

A Danzig whom he should never have trusted.

The members of the expedition had changed places with the convicts, for freed, eager hands had thrust Hanson's people into the dark, cavernous hold. The canvas hatch cover had been slammed back into position, and the Borgheses, Laura Travis, Charley Adams, Jacobs, Kuan, Jan, Toshi and her girls, as well as the ship's crew, were all imprisoned, subject to Lester Danzig's next whim. The elder Borghese was the one restless member of the new order of things. He was pacing back and forth like a caged lion, pausing only to ask the dazed Rigby how he felt. The young scientist was still considerably under the weather after his ordeal in the diving bell. Laura Travis sat as still as death. Only the cloud of sorrow and anxiety in her lovely eyes indicated what she was feeling. Toshi and Leoncavallo were holding hands in the semigloom, trying to draw warmth and comfort from each other. Charley Adams stared at the closed hatch cover, her thoughts on what was happening to Harry Connerly. Hanson's officers, Jacobs specifically, were sour-faced and worried. The thunderous rumble of the nearby Krakatoa lent an aura of doom to their new situation. The running and stamping of the convicts' chained feet pounded intermittently overhead, pierced by cries and shouts of exaltation and anger. This did little to make anyone feel any better. There was uneasiness and dread in the close atmosphere of the hatch.

Giovanni Borghese paused in his pacing to crouch concernedly over Douglas Rigby.

"How do you feel?"

"All right."

Borghese nodded, his eyes looking upward toward the commotion topside.

"They run like animals released from cages."

Douglas Rigby pressed his fingers against his throbbing temples. The heat of the hold was unbearable.

"Small wonder that they would. . . ."

Borghese had nothing to say to that. He resumed his pacing.

All men resemble wild beasts when they are caged.

Danzig was standing on the closed portion of the hatch. Next to him was the battered, still-damp safe, its door bent and dangling open. The burn marks where Hanson's acetylene torch had eaten home shone ugly in the hazy sunlight. Danzig's bearded, grimy face was tightened into a victorious grimace. The pistol was prominent in his waistband, handle jutting within easy reach.

The winch had stopped squealing. Harry Connerly's limp, rubber-suited body had been lowered into the hold. Hanson, whom Danzig wanted, had remained behind. Two convicts had stripped him of his weighted shoes, gloves and steel helmet. All about the steaming deck, Danzig's convicts cavorted, spitting over the side into the sea, grinning like monkeys in the sunlight, shaking their fists at mighty Krakatoa standing behind the port rail, cursing all the authority in the universe. Hanson watched with silent fury, seeing how very close indeed the human is to the animal. The wheelhouse had been taken over by a trio of bearded, sweaty convicts who were taking turns playing with the steam whistle of the *Batavia Queen*. The shrill blasts punctured the somber silence of the bay. Krakatoa seemed to rumble back in angry response. Danzig barked an order to the men on the bridge, and the whistle stopped blasting.

Hanson was propelled by two of the convicts toward Danzig. The heavy diving suit, even without weights and accessories, was cumbersome. Hanson's lean face bore the marks of perspiration, strain and discomfort. Danzig's eyes flicked over him, absorbing his reaction to the mutiny. He was all business now. There was no gloating in his manner. This had been a necessary action. He was trying to convey that to Hanson without putting it into words; only his smile was ghoulish.

He pointed a finger toward the safe, stepping to one side so that Hanson could see.

"Look!" he rasped.

"Lester," Hanson began. "If I were—"

He was suddenly shoved hard from behind. He stumbled forward and Danzig caught him, holding him up, compelling him to look into the partially open safe. Hanson stared.

The twisted door obscured most of the interior. Danzig shot out a hand, tugging the barrier toward himself so that Hanson could get a good look. The shelves were awry. Hanson made out some soggy articles: virtually disintegrated papers, a book, an oilskin-wrapped logbook, a rusty, ornate letter opener in the form of intertwining angels and a small nondescript pocket watch. That was all.

There was nothing else to be seen save the rust, age and

decaying condition of a large steel object that has been underwater for a great length of time.

"That's it," Danzig cursed. "That's everything that was in there." His voice was a disgusted grate of sound. He leaned against the safe.

"A lousy watch," he continued.

Hanson smiled bleakly.

"Petty theft. Hardly up to your standard, Lester."

Danzig's face hardened. The killer in him showed through his eyes.

"I take what people are too weak to keep, that's all. Whether it's three days' deck privileges or . . . a cheap watch."

On the word, he leaned into the interior of the safe, reaching. Hanson uncoiled. He swung the heavy door closed with all his force, virtually chopping Danzig in half. Danzig cried out in agony. Hanson snatched the pistol from his waist before he could be stopped. The two convicts, loitering behind him, came on with a rush, heavy chains swinging. One lifted his wrist links for a crushing blow. Hanson had little choice. He fired quickly. The shot drove flush into the man's stomach; he went down with surprise and terror upon his face. Hanson whirled, dodging the other man. Convicts, alerted and outraged, closed in from every direction. The only opening was toward the winch. He started for it, sluggishly because of the suit. Danzig rose from behind the iron safe, the ornate letter opener clutched in his right hand. Danzig's expression was terrible. An amalgam of agony and sheer hatred.

Hanson triggered the pistol again from a distance of only three feet. Danzig twisted, the bullet hurling him backward into the dark interior of the safe. He crumpled, an awkward rag doll of a man now blasted into sudden death, with an iron coffin his whether he wanted it or not. But it was still not over for Hanson. Swirling, onrushing gray-clad figures were trying to overwhelm him, coming on with any kind of weapon they could lay their hands on—belaying pins, wooden buckets, wrist irons, random clubs and truncheons or their own legs. Hanson fired twice more. Two convicts went down and their cronies climbed over them. Hanson lumbered toward the winch, gaining it, just as a convict attempted to turn the steam hose his way. Hanson's next shot caught the man in the chest. As the derelict toppled, Hanson caught up the powerful hose, kicking the handle as he came. The snake of rubber tubing hissed and roared. A blast of scalding steam funneled from the nozzle. Screams and a mad scramble filled the air. The scorching breath of the steam had found a handful of victims. It was a terrible weapon to use but the incredible odds in combat dismissed the niceties of fair play. Hanson held fast behind the hose, advancing slowly, directing the steam. The convicts fell back to a man. The more frightened ones hurled themselves over the side into the sea; others first fled in panic, then plummeted over the side. In his grotesque costume, Hanson was like some relentless god from the deep.

A few hardier souls had dropped the lifeboat. Swimming men took off after the retreating craft as oars dipped with insensate savagery.

Others swam for the shore, as if the looming Krakatoa were their destination. Soon, Hanson was on the deck alone. Virtually alone, save for the dead bodies and the mute legs of Lester Danzig poking from his iron coffin, the helpless feet pointing toward the hazy sky. Hanson shook himself, dropping the hose. For a long moment, he took a deep breath. Silence reigned on the decks of the *Batavia Queen*.

With the still-loaded pistol in his hand, Hanson moved like a dead man toward the canvas-covered hold. His eyes were two bloodshot balls of weariness and spent stamina. His arms and legs felt like lifeless weights.

The furled rigging of the ship creaked and groaned in a mild offshore breeze playing in the ratlines. A seagull suddenly cawed above the mizzenmast, its white wings flapping like a window shade. Hanson smiled. A tired, sad smile.

At least the mutiny, such as it was, was over.

The awful revelation that the safe did not hold what the entire expedition had been all about was another matter entirely.

A very sad, very hopeless matter.

Slowly, every movement an effort, Hanson poised over the hatch cover. It was time to let his private goldfish out of their bowl.

At least, he could give them back their freedom.

They gathered around him, staring into the all but empty interior of the underwater safe. All the expressions on their faces were as bleak as the safe's interior. Laura Travis had quickly retrieved the sturdily wrapped logbook. She moved away from the group, unwrapping it very carefully, her head lowered.

Douglas Rigby let the sopping papers dribble out of his hands as the Borgheses watched him.

"Our treasure," Rigby said sadly.

"One fifth," Giovanni Borghese muttered, "of nothing."

Krakatoa grumbled again, as if underscoring the futility and helplessness of man. But this time there was a greater volume of smoke, a flare of fireballs, accompanying the restless sounds.

Charley Adams had taken Harry Connerly back to his cabin.

Hanson and Laura stood in the large salon. The logbook was spread on the table before them. Laura was frowning; the frown the beginning of tears coursing down her exquisitely soft and lovely face. They were alone.

"Nothing, Chris. Not-one-thing." She was shaken.

Hanson, cool and clean in white cotton shirt and trousers, confirmed her worry. But he was quickly leafing through the preceding pages which had occupied her attention.

"He put into port once . . . Palembang Point."

"But no mention of Peter!" Her voice rose hysterically.

Hanson ignored that, studying a page of the volume closely, tracing with a finger the penned lines. Travis' hand was the firm, disciplined penmanship of an authoritative man.

"And when he got word of the hurricane he ran toward Krakatoa for a safer anchorage. But what was he doing at Palembang?"

"Oh, Chris." She was near breaking now. "It's hopeless. I shouldn't have come. It was wrong to give me hope."

"Maybe there's something earlier in the log. Some kind of . . ." He paused, for his thumb racing through the pages had come upon something. A scrap of paper, then other scraps. He discarded them as soon as he had glanced over them. Finally, he came upon an envelope. A pale blue envelope. Laura Travis gasped.

He raised the letter. There was a name and address in childish script on the outside. The letter was unpostmarked, obviously unmailed. He passed the letter to Laura. She took it, her tearful eyes unbelieving.

"To me . . ." she said in a hushed whisper. "From Peter."

"Read it."

She ripped it open, unfolding it with trembling hands. As she began to read it to herself, the Borgheses and Douglas Rigby filed into the salon quietly. An air of depression hung over them. Giovanni Borghese smiled thinly at Hanson.

"Krakatoa is about to go off, Captain Hanson. I suggest we do the same."

Neither Hanson nor Laura seemed to notice their presence. Hanson was watching Laura, waiting to hear what she would say.

"He . . . misses me. He . . . he's being sent to school. . . ." Tearfully, she was picking up the salient points of the letter. "At Palembang . . . Chris, at Palembang!" Greatly excited, daring to hope again, her eyes flew to Hanson. She crumpled the letter to her bosom and embraced him, holding him feverishly.

Then Hanson whirled, freeing himself, darting for the stairs that led to the bridge. Rigby called bewilderedly after him. "Palembang?"

Over his shoulder, Hanson shouted, "That's where we're going."

"Where's that?" Leoncavallo blurted.

"I'll show you."

The three men sprinted after him. Laura Travis gathered up the logbook, wiping her eyes. She followed the men out, her heart beating with hope and love. She walked with new spirit. The dead had come back. Both herself and Peter Travis.

Hanson was at the rail, facing Krakatoa when the Borgheses and Douglas Rigby caught up with him. They lined the rail beside him. Hanson pointed a finger toward the spewing volcano. They saw the rocky channel which passed directly in the path of Krakatoa. Narrow, walled, treacherous; a tunnel-like entrance.

"Your pearls are right through there," Hanson said grimly.

He left them with that, hurrying toward the bridge ladder. Giovanni Borghese frowned at his son. Douglas Rigby shook his head. None of the three men could quite digest the captain's cryptic information. It seemed absurd, on the face of it.

Laura Travis had moved up behind them, still clasping the logbook. The men did not notice her. They were transfixed, their eyes on the frightening aperture below Krakatoa which Hanson had indicated as the route toward the treasure.

The fury of the volcano seemed more awesome than ever.

"We'll go into it at dead slow," Hanson told Jacobs and Kuan inside the wheelhouse. Both officers showed only the barest reaction at the incredible order. "Mr. Jacobs, get everyone under cover. Passengers, crew, everybody. I want the decks cleared."

Jacobs stirred. "Shall I set up a fire watch?"

"Absolutely. Kuan, go out on the starboard bridge and keep a lookout."

Jacobs left the wheelhouse and Kuan, signaling the engine room telegraph first, left too. Hanson rubbed his hands together, his eyes silently acknowledging the menace of Krakatoa, ominously close. He would get closer, too. In all his savage splendor.

The *Batavia Queen* shuddered with fresh movement. The winch hissed into life. The stern propellors churned, white wake foaming noisily. The anchor chain started to clank upward from the green bed it lay in. The ship began its slow, steady turn, the prow aimed toward Krakatoa. Fire and smoke pumped steadily from the volcano, seemingly blotting out that portion of the sky. The vessel steamed forward. Gathering speed until it hit the dead-slow level Hanson had urged. Daylight was waning, the skies looking leaden and heavy.

The crew, solemn and wary and mindful of the nearness of the tremendous natural monster filling their eyes, drenched down the hatch canvas with buckets of water. The ship was moving slowly, directly beneath the foot of the cliffs approaching Krakatoa. The dangerous passage, the hazardously jagged channel of rocks lining its side, waited for the prow of the ship to enter. Hanson, vigilant at the wheel, steadied his course. The *Batavia Queen* plowed through the entrance mouth of the passage. Krakatoa groaned mightily, lava and hot air laying an ashen mist across the hull of the vessel.

Jacobs had quietly and efficiently hustled the passengers to safety, urging them below decks with orders to stay there. No one protested Hanson's edict. If anything, their own eyes told them what Hanson meant. From the salon windows where they huddled, they could see the sheer rocky walls of the canyon passage rising on both starboard and port. It was an uncannily weird sensation; a feeling of being boxed in, suffocated. And then there was the now almost unbearable, stifling atmosphere. The fierce stench of burning sulfur, the noxious fumes of flaming lava and minerals of perhaps unknown origin. The air was filled with the grinding, jarring roar of the volcano overhead. Laura Travis and Douglas Rigby had already been in the salon. They remained at Jacobs' request while he went to direct the others. Rigby was still too worn from his ordeal in the diving bell to protest. As for Laura, she said nothing.

In the passageway, Jacobs encountered Charley Adams.

"The captain asks you to stay in your cabin, Miss."

"Don't worry!" Charley darted back into her room, fear speeding her in.

From the wheelhouse window, Hanson kept his eyes straight ahead. The burning air, the falling shreds of molten lava, made the view uncertain. A fireball arched into the sea, shooting sparks. Down the precipitous sides of the rocky gorge, rolling lava poured, extinguishing itself in the waters. Jan, the helmsman, stood at the forward portside window, trembling. Hanson flung him a reassuring glance, as if he welcomed the challenge of Krakatoa; this slipping by his very doorstep, unscathed.

Another fireball hit the deck, disintegrating, the shreds richocheting in all directions. Jan jerked with the impact as if he could feel it. Kuan hurried in from the starboard deck. His bland face was worried.

"We're running pretty close, starboard, Captain."

A tremendous crash, jarring the wheelhouse roof, followed on the words. Jan and Kuan ducked involuntarily. Hanson laughed harshly. "Fireball. Check overhead!"

Kuan and Jan fled from the wheelhouse to look at the damage. Hanson steadily held the ship on course, allowing for Kuan's fast report.

In Connerly's cabin, Charley Adams was gape-mouthed at the porthole. Everything was so dark; she could barely make out Harry in his bunk.

"Harry, it's pitch black all of a sudden. It's daytime but there's just darkness . . . and fire. . . ."

Connerly, lost in his failure below the sea, could only stare up at the cabin ceiling. He felt more dead than alive. The dangerous gamble that Hanson was taking meant nothing to him. Not all the fires of hell and damnation could burn away his disgust with himself.

The *Batavia Queen* was running through the passage now. Plowing steadily, steaming, moving right along. Hanson held the wheel firm. The ship was passing directly beneath the peak of Krakatoa, at last. The awful peak, shrouded in violent colors, was raining down all the molten debris at its command, as if openly waging war on the trespasser in his midst.

Jacobs burst into the wheelhouse, his face agitated, his uniform crumpled. Hanson shot him a quick side glance.

"Kuan says you're cutting it pretty close, starboard."

"I mean to," Hanson said calmly.

The first officer shrugged, taking Jan's position at the portside window. Jan moved to the engine room telegraph, as if by command.

"Passengers all secure. Crew on fire watch," Jacobs said.

Hanson nodded, still staring intently forward. The reddish haze of flame and lava ash hung like a curtain before the steaming prow of the ship. A rain of flaming rocks, like a star shower, cascaded down on the open decks before him. The decks were suddenly obscured with fire and smoke as the wood ignited. Hanson cursed. The hit was directly over the chain locker room where the diving girls were located.

In the smoke-filled salon where thin wisps curled down from the deck stairs, Laura Travis was too nervous to read any more from the logbook. Douglas Rigby, desperately trying to see out of a porthole, suddenly headed for the stairs. As he mounted them rapidly, he called out to Laura. Half in apology, half in explanation.

"Sorry. I just have to be where I can watch. It's the most exciting thing I've ever . . . *almost* seen."

He galloped up the stairway. She didn't try to stop him. She understood what Hanson meant about him now.

He was one of those sorts of men who always has to see what is on the other side of the mountain. Come hell or high water.

She was now alone in the salon.

Alone with the smoke, the thunder, the flames and her own very frightened self.

Toshi and the girls, Kiko, Midori and Sumi, cowered in the chain locker opening. The air had suddenly come alive with licking flames and searing heat. Awful noises cannonaded on the ceiling over their heads. They could hear the sounds of running feet. The crew on deck, desperately rushing back and forth to extinguish small deadly fires springing up all over the *Batavia Queen*. Toshi tried to smile, to alleviate the misery of her companions, but she could not. Mighty Krakatoa of legend and the very fiber of their lives was angry with them. He had spoken and he would be heard. Toshi tried not to be frightened but she was; where was Leoncavallo? Was he all right?

The vivid colors, the spewing rock and flame, lit up the face of Krakatoa. The yawning canyon below was like a ready-made receptacle eager to receive the tribute of lava, rock and fireball. The pitifully tiny ship, buffeted from all sides, pushed feebly through the smoke-filled, flame-lit nightmare.

A burning rock resting on the hatch glowed like a beacon. Hissing smoke and fusing materials burst into blaze. The crew hurried to combat the new menace.

On the starboard bridge, Kuan cupped his hands and roared through the haze toward the wheelhouse. *"Coral head!"* Hanson cut the wheel sharply to port. Jacobs pointed, shouting too. The din was incredible. Hanson's eyes and ears ached.

"I see it!" Jacobs bellowed. "About twenty-five yards dead ahead!" The *Queen* gradually altered course, slipping by the coral formation by inches. Jacobs and Jan exchanged sweaty, relieved glances. Hanson swung the wheel back to midships. He made no comment. None was necessary.

Douglas Rigby, shadowing the route of the ship, had gained the rail overlooking the forward hatch. Wonderment was etched on his face. He had no time for fear. The fascination with the pagan, primordial behavior of Krakatoa pushed aside all other considerations. He watched in awe as the volcano shot a sheet of flame skyward. A tremendous geyser of fury, coordinated with a bursting thunderclap of sound from the peak. Rigby strained his eyes. He could just distinguish the calm, illuminated surface of the waters ahead. Only falling debris dappled the tranquil end mouth of the passage Hanson had chosen for his perilous journey.

Rigby roved the smoking decks of the ship, dodging the running seamen, busy with the multitude of fires. At portside, a meteoric fireball whooshed with startling suddenness directly before his feet. Rigby fell back, terrified. He recoiled against a protective bulkhead. The hatch had splintered, a smoking hole indicating the path of the fireball cutting through the timbers.

Behind him, Kuan swept by, other shapes following him. It was hard to make anything out very accurately in the haze.

"Get below!" he heard Kuan yelling at the men. "It broke through!" The black giant from Trinidad, Squid, loomed at his side.

Pulled from his scientific detachment, Rigby hurried back to the main salon. Crashing, splintering noises followed him as he ducked down the stairs. Laura Travis, alone in the salon, had drawn back in panic from the blazing dining table. The massive tablecloth was burning crisply, igniting the center of the room. The conflagration threatened to spread throughout the salon, and then the entire ship. Rigby, heedless of the danger and mindful of the lovely frightened creature that needed him, hurried forward, ripping the tablecloth free. Laura herself did not remain helpless for long. A pair of silver ice buckets stood on the wooden bar, still holding partially filled champagne and wine bottles. With Rigby's assistance, she made quick, expert use of them. There was also a large dishpan full of glasses, awash in dirty water. Rigby grinned tightly as he and Laura slowly suffocated the flaming fireball which had landed in the heart of the room. The water extinguished the blaze, with the added help of flailing bar towels and window drapes and pillows, all dampened with the remainder of the water.

Finally, faces and hands blackened from their efforts, Rigby and Laura subsided wearily into chairs. Wearily but victoriously.

They had saved the salon.

At least, temporarily.

The constant, drumming cannonading of Krakatoa filled the narrow confines of the chain locker entrance. Clouds of sulfurous smoke drifted above the heads of Toshi and the girls. Midori was crying softly. Toshi comforted her. Through the opaque mist, she could imagine the voice of Leoncavallo calling to her from the bridge or from somewhere—she wasn't sure. The din was so confusing, so terrible. The intense heat made the flesh crawl. Now Toshi was startled anew. *"Toshi!"* There was no mistake. Leoncavallo was calling her. Quickly the girl moved forward, motioning her friends to keep still, to wait.

She moved out of the protection of the chain locker. She took one step, and then another. She looked up. The sight was awesome and spectacular. Krakatoa, the blazing mists, and yet the sky seemed devoid of fireballs and flying debris for one peaceful moment. Toshi walked out on deck.

Her heart quickened as she saw Leoncavallo and his father up on the second deck, just above the hatch. Leoncavallo was still shouting her name, and his father was trying to pull him back to the safety of the bridge. Toshi started forward, to go up to meet them.

Leoncavallo must not worry about her. Joyfully, she would let him know she was safe and well—

"Toshi!" came the forlorn, desperate shout of her name again.

She ran forward.

A fireball abruptly crashed onto the hatch in front of her

and bounded into the open sea. She stopped, frightened. She looked up, trembling. Her tiny figure was like a lost child's.

A series of comets, speeding like flaming arrows, whirled over the decks of the *Batavia Queen*. Toshi, terrified into trancelike fear, backed slowly along the rail. She could not take her eyes off the destroying sky. From the bridge, Kuan stared down at the defenseless girl, unable to cry out. Hanson appeared; he had seen everything from the wheelhouse. Borghese's struggle to keep Leoncavallo from running into the blazing hold and the stupid, senseless act of the girl, putting herself in a position of danger.

The girl stood transfixed by the fireballs in the sky, the brilliant flashes of light illuminating her piquant lovely face. The wide-set eyes were two pools of terror. And incomprehension. And wonder.

Hanson shouted to her to go back to the chain locker. She tried to turn, to look. She moved slowly. Like an automaton. But the chain locker was almost obliterated from view by smoke and whirling tongues of fire.

Leoncavallo broke free of Borghese's hold. Just in time to see everything and be able to do nothing. A sudden blinding flash of light bathed the deck with the intensity of daylight. An arcing fireball, blazing, exploding, phosphorescent, thundered down from the sky. The place where Toshi stood, rooted in terror, disappeared in a blasting, bursting ball of flame.

Leoncavallo staggered back, shocked speechless. His father caught him in his arms, clasped him feverishly, burying his face in the boy's shoulder. Leoncavallo stared, unseeing, at the mad world about them.

"Borghese!" Hanson whipped out, running by. "Keep him here!" A husky crewman, sensing the situation, moved quickly to Borghese's side. Leoncavallo was beginning to squirm and struggle hysterically, shouting Toshi's name, crying his hurt to the world that had gone mad. Borghese, his eyes brimming with tears, helped the seaman subdue his overwrought son.

Hanson skidded to a halt at the top of the stairs. The flaming object below made him turn away in horror and hopelessness. The fused, twisted deck was a rising sheet of flame in which nothing could have survived. Another fireball slammed down, close to Hanson, forcing him back up the ladder. The fierce heat licked out at him, burning him, singeing his hair; it was useless to go on.

At the chain locker entrance, the three girl divers stared stonily midships. Sumi suddenly whirled and buried her face in Midori's shoulder. Kiko, dry-eyed, gazed up at Krakatoa, her lips moving in a blasphemous indictment.

Hanson returned to the Borgheses and the seaman who held the boy locked in his powerful arms.

"Please go below," he said. There was a trace of emotion in his voice that Giovanni Borghese had never heard. "I'll . . . do what I can."

Jan was at the wheel. Jacobs stood at the window, watching the dreadful sight below. Suddenly his attention was diverted by something ahead of the *Batavia Queen* to port. The sheer sides of the narrow, volcanic passage had been loosened by eroding lava fissures. Even as he watched, the wall toppled forward, creating a landslide of molten lava. Jan had seen it, too. He cut the wheel sharply to starboard. The tremendous, metallic lurching of the ship flung the men on her decks about like loose belaying pins. A great shout of dismay went up.

The exit from the passage was blocked. The ship was angled dangerously in the channel, her prow wedged to starboard. Jan had done all that could be done to avert a catastrophe. Hanson came charging up the rungs of the bridge ladder. He flung into the wheelhouse and took the wheel from Jan. His face was stony, bleak.

"Full astern!" he ordered.

"Full astern!" Jan moved the telegraph arm with a noisy clang.

Hanson kept the wheel on starboard.

The ship's propellor reversed direction, chopping the water rapidly. The *Batavia Queen* began to back off the rocks, limping with the effort.

"Dead slow ahead!" Hanson barked.

"Dead slow!" Jan repeated.

Krakatoa issued another shuddering roar as the vessel navigated very carefully past the rocky blockade.

The choking, lung-searing air made it difficult to breathe. Hanson sighed.

"I wonder what the hell we did to the bottom. Frank?"

"I'll check," Jacobs said. His all-in-a-day's-work attitude always had a sobering effect on Hanson. It was good to have a first officer who didn't fold up in emergencies.

Nor was he a Lester Danzig, thank the Lord.

A flaming fireball had crashed into the cavernous cargo storage, landing not far from *Butterfly III*. Scorching fingers of fire licked out at the steel sides of the bell. Flames shot upward, threatening the stored crates and bales of cargo. Hanson's crew, smoke-blackened and maddened by the holocaust that now seemed endless, raced up and down ladders, doing battle. Jacobs and two sailors carrying lanterns stopped momentarily to observe the seamen fighting the blaze. Satisfied, Jacobs directed his two men to open a metal hatch in the steel decking. The bilge proved to be filled with a couple of feet of blackened water in a cramped space. The men with the lanterns dripped along the hull, checking the metal plates of the ship. The throb of the engine room sounded very close. The *Batavia Queen*, summoning all her steam power, was edging forward through the continuous hail of fire, lava and smoke. The wrenching sounds from above spurred the crew on, making them work faster and harder.

In the wheelhouse, Hanson and Jan had their hands full. The volcano had saved something up for them all. A deadly rain of rock missiles now pelted the ship, smashing the rigging, breaking through the battered smokestack. Krakatoa had not done with them yet, even though the exit from the passage was closer than ever. Hanson could see the flat sea beyond the carnage of the volcanic upheaval.

"Shoals to port," Jan said, watchful at the wheelhouse window. Hanson tucked the wheel a few points to starboard. The ship was still responding to his touch, although sluggishly. She had taken the fiercest beating of her life with perhaps more yet to come.

Jacobs emerged from the bridge.

"No bottom damage," he reported. "Fire in the forward hatch is under control."

"Good. We're almost clear now. Kuan!"

Kuan appeared as if by magic. Hanson smiled. He had a good crew. Fine officers.

"Wet down fore and aft. Get a sounding."

"Yes, sir."

The ship stirred, men running and shouting again. Sight of the exit had kindled the spark of life. Hanson watched the men run to the foresails, dousing them with water from the wooden buckets. Near the rail, a seaman slung a lead line into the water, measuring the depth of the fatal passage.

"By the mark five fathoms!" the cry echoed up to the bridge.

"I wonder what Palembang's gonna look like," Jacobs mused, almost to himself.

"We'll know in a minute," Hanson said.

On the portside, the first outlines of land shone through the remainder of the ash-laden, smoky mist from the anger of Krakatoa. Hanson nodded to himself and pulled the whistle cord. The rumbling, growling thunder of the mountain echoed threateningly from the stern of the *Batavia Queen*.

In the salon, Laura Travis and Douglas Rigby looked at one another, reacting to the sudden sounding of the ship's whistle. They hurried out of the room.

In Connerly's cabin, Charley Adams threw her arms around Harry's neck and cried out happily.

"Harry, Harry! We made it!"

"Yeah," Harry Connerly said, still looking at the ceiling.

In their cabin, the Borgheses hardly heard the sound. Leoncavallo wept and Giovanni Borghese stared miserably at the floor of the room.

In the chain locker, Kiko, Midori and Sumi joined in a traditional, silent prayer for their dead comrade, Toshi.

Among the many seamen battling the blazes that still threatened to damn the good ship *Batavia Queen*, the giant black seaman from Trinidad, Squid, worked more powerfully and furiously than any two men.

He hadn't believed it possible, but Captain Hanson had licked the mighty Krakatoa!

Palembang was in ruins.

With the ship at dead slow, Hanson surveyed the destruction from the portside bridge. The sight was chilling, as such devastation is even to the hardest-hearted, thickest-skinned man. The gods might laugh, the elements cry out, but nothing on earth could match the furious senseless onslaught of the Furies. Palembang had been struck by worse than lightning.

The once verdant, now smoking jungle, saturated with rushing lava, sent climbing clouds of flame to the skies. The entire area of foliage and settlement houses was razed to the ground. The first buildings seen from the deck were ablaze or already charred ruins. The frame shack school, the chapel house, the native huts—nothing had escaped the fiery hand of Krakatoa. The horizon was a burnt ember of fused colors. There was movement all along the shore; figures racing through the jungle to escape destruction. Hanson brought a telescope to bear, picking up Malays in headlong flight, children in their arms, their few possessions left behind or discarded in the underbrush. Hanson's jaw muscles hardened at the pitiful sight.

Laura Travis and Douglas Rigby appeared at his elbow. He could hear Laura's shocked, whimpering voice. "It's gone! Burned!" Hanson did not have to ask her what she meant. Nor did Rigby. The flamed-out schoolhouse stood mute and skeletal beyond the beach. All Palembang was in ashes. Nothing had escaped.

Beyond the center of the destroyed village, a wavering shadow moved along the shoreline: the outline of a Chinese junk, green-sailed and indistinct in the haze, pulling away from the smoking wooden dock.

Hanson, alert as ever, went into the wheelhouse. There was nothing to say to Laura now. Now was only the time for action. Weeping never brought anyone or anything back.

"A junk just pulled away from the dock," he told Jan. "Come along starboard." Jan nodded, spinning the wheel. A full turn to port. Hanson reached for a megaphone and returned to the bridge. He still couldn't look at Laura.

At the rail, he peered closely through the smoke, making out the other boat. It was very close now. It would have touched the bowsprit of the *Batavia Queen* save for Hanson's watchdog scrutiny. The junk swung out, coming alongside, starboard.

"Stop engines!" Hanson bellowed.

Through the megaphone, he shouted to the boat below. The smoke was still thick, swirling, but he could make out the Chinese skipper standing at the rail. The doomed island of Palembang continued burning in the background.

"Do you need help?" Hanson called down.

The voice answering back was shrill, urgent.

"No help . . . hurry . . . go."

"Where are the people from the mission?"

"Take other boat. All gone."

"And the children from the school?"

"All same. Gone this morning."

Hanson paused only a second. It was an eerie dialogue, talking with a man one could barely see.

"Where?"

"Java," the Chinese skipper singsonged.

"What kind of boat?"

There was no answer this time. It was useless to go on. The junk, eager to quit the island, had continued on its flight through the concealing smoke. Hanson set the megaphone aside. He found Laura staring at him, her eyes showing that glimmer of hope again. He smiled at her briefly, calling over his shoulder to the wheelhouse.

"Come to one-six-five and hold it!" To Laura, he said very softly, "Java."

The tiny junk vanished completely into the distance. The bow of the *Batavia Queen* turned seaward. Along the shore, the gutted settlement of Palembang Point receded slowly from view. It was like leaving behind a very bad dream.

Almost, but not quite.

Leoncavallo slumped against the porthole of the Borghese cabin. He was exhausted, physically and emotionally. His youthful face, set in lines of grief, was dirt-smeared and tragic. On the bunk opposite him sat Giovanni Borghese, coatless, his tie loosened, his usual grand air completely gone. A tray with a pitcher of water and two glasses lay on the floor.

Borghese poured the remaining few drops of water into one of the glasses and extended it to his son.

"Water, Leoncavallo?"

The young man shook his head. His voice was weary and hollow when he answered. "I am almost talked-out now, I think."

Borghese smiled, though there was sadness in the expression.

"Thank you for telling me of her. Thank you for caring . . . to tell me. Remarkable, this girl."

Leoncavallo suddenly moved to the chest of drawers behind him, sloshing water from the basin there, across his heated face.

"What I haven't told you yet," he said, "concerns us."

"Oh?" Borghese was surprised at that.

Leoncavallo nodded, evidently chosing his words with great care. "When I realized my feelings for Toshi, I tried very hard to make her like me as much as I did her. I tried being charming. I showed all the manners I'd ever learned, told little implausible stories to interest her, impress her. I was —" He paused. "I was *you*."

Borghese nodded sympathetically, knowingly, but he could not take his eyes off his son's earnest face.

"It wasn't even I who noticed it. *She* did."

"What did she say?" Borghese asked slowly.

"She said—" Memory was obviously very painful, very

rueful. "She touched my face and she said . . . be yourself. It is *this* Borghese I love."

His father said wonderingly, "Such a perceptive young girl. She cared for you very much, Leoncavallo."

"After that, for the first time I was not in competition with you anymore. It was a great weight from my shoulders, Poppa."

"It is very satisfying being one's self and still being liked, is it not?"

"And what good does it do me?" Leoncavallo muttered bitterly. "What have I got left?"

The older man frowned, snapping at him sharply. Self-pity was never the answer. Never the way of the Borgheses.

"Leoncavallo! You've got your life."

They looked at each other, father and son, for a long important moment. Then the sound of the ship's whistle intruded almost urgently.

Neither of them could know at the time that the bridge had sighted a sampan with tattered sails.

A sampan crowded full of people.

"What is it?" Hanson asked, responding to the whistle.

"There," Jacobs said as Kuan passed Hanson the telescope. The sampan was small, broad-beamed, shredded sails hanging limply in the dead wind. The mass of humanity on board, indistinguishable from the bridge of the *Batavia Queen*, writhed like a nameless monster. Through the ash-laden atmosphere, visibility was still poor.

Laura Travis, spent and tired but still clinging to her dreams, murmured feebly at Hanson's elbow. "Is it . . . ?" Silently, he handed her the glass.

Kuan grunted. "We were watching. Whenever they stop bailing, she starts to list."

Laura could see that was true. The sampan was foundering badly. A sea of faces, all ages, swam in the glass. She shook her head helplessly. It was so difficult to see.

"Too far to tell?" Hanson asked.

"Yes," she said regretfully.

"Whoever they are, they're in trouble. Jacobs, drop the starboard lifeboat. Get a ladder over the side. Kuan, break out the diving platform."

The sampan was filled to the gunwhales with children, nuns, priests, crewmen and even small dogs. Hanson could hear the medley of anguished cries and howls carrying across the water. As Jacobs and Kuan organized the men for a rescue party, Hanson swept the telescope across the sampan.

Men were bailing furiously, the terrified passengers recoiling from the slosh of seawater filling the broad-beamed vessel. To Hanson's smoke-reddened eye it was another scene from hell. Laura Travis tugged impatiently at his elbow. Hanson suddenly checked the telescope, holding it firmly on one position in the boat. Unless he was seeing things, the glass had picked up a familiar sight. A small, dark, handsome child. A boy of perhaps eight. Hanson stared for a moment before passing the glass to Laura once more.

He watched her.

Her expression didn't change for several seconds and then he saw her lips silently form the name *Peter*. She was virtually unbelieving, not daring to believe less she be dashed down once more. But no, it was true. She was saying the boy's name aloud now, alternating tears of happiness and murmurs of prayers.

"Peter! It *is*, Chris! You found him!"

He nodded slowly. At least, there was one thing successful about the voyage. Peter Travis had been found. Alive.

Jacobs, compassionately observing the life-and-death struggle on the sampan, moved closer to Hanson, speaking quietly to him.

"She may not stay afloat long enough, Chris. She's already settled some since we sighted her."

In answer, Hanson seized his megaphone, strode to the rail and bellowed to his crew standing midships, watching the drama unfold. A whiplash of command was in his tone.

"Any crewman who can swim, get to that boat! Get the people off!" Swinging toward the stern, he shouted: "Hurry that lifeboat!"

Activities aboard the *Queen* became prodigious. The men, aroused and anxious to do something, dove from the railing in every direction, striking out for the crippled boat. The lifeboat, creaking and groaning, lowered swiftly into the sea. The divers' cage swung out over the side, the winch propelling the platform. Both Borgheses, father and son, were aboard. Ready to do all they could to help.

Swimming seamen flecked the water between the two craft now. Yet it was all too clear that Jacobs' prediction was true. The sampan was foundering and a mass scramble of humanity spilled over its sides into the sea. The children, the nuns, the priests. Peter Travis was among them. Soon the waters were a wriggling, paddling, churning tide of swimming human flotsam. The seamen stroking from the *Queen* and the survivors swimming from the sampan boiled the sea into a giant cauldron.

Hanson stood at the rail, waiting to direct operations. Douglas Rigby climbed down the rope ladder suspended from the deck, ready to assist all survivors and to help in any way he could. Laura Travis stayed at Hanson's side, her eyes searching the oncoming faces of the victims of another calamity at sea. The rescue work was just beginning to show results, Hanson's men towing people back from death. The ladder became crowded. Rigby had his hands full, passing up children, cowled nuns and aged priests. One of the children clutched a small black dog, his eyes shining with excitement. But this was not Peter Travis. Laura waited, her heart beating like a drum.

Giovanni and Leoncavallo Borghese tugged children and adults from the water, stacking the divers' platform with a cargo of wet, grateful humanity. In the near distance, Krakatoa sent up a spiral of ocher smoke, shuddering deeply again. Forebodingly. Hanson shot the volcano a curious look, his eyes narrowing.

The lifeboat alongside the sinking sampan was filling up fast. There were yells and shouts of gratitude, mingled with more cries of fear.

Rigby had his hands full on the boarding ladder. The Borgheses, with a complete load on the platform, signaled the winch operator, and the loaded cage swayed dangerously as it was brought over the deck. In the water, more people were coming.

One of these was the boy, Peter Travis. Hanson could pick out his plucky face from the mass. The boy was a fine swimmer.

Luggage, belongings, crates, boxes and possessions were handed off the sampan into the lifeboat, loading it to the maximum.

Rigby reached down for the dark-haired youngster, assisting him up the first rungs. The boy climbed readily, handily, a scampering monkey. For he had seen his mother, Laura Travis, at the head of the ladder, waiting with shining eyes. Peter Travis fell into her arms. She smothered him, all the yearning and lost hope soothed with the tremendous balm of the knowledge that he was not dead, but alive and well and here in her arms. Hanson looked on, the back of his neck suddenly tingling. He brushed at his eyes impatiently.

"Let me look at you. Oh, Peter, let me see you . . ."

"Mother . . ."

"Peter, Peter . . ."

An ear-to-ear grin made the little-boy face lopsided. Peter Travis was overcome with joy.

Charley Adams, in the vicinity of the boarding ladder, felt a warm glow. Harry Connerly stared out at the sea. The lifeboat pulled toward the ship with cargo and sailors jammed together. Rigby, at the base of the ladder, drew a tiny, wet Chinese boy up from the arms of a sailor. The boy screamed his displeasure and fright. Rigby smiled.

The divers' platform, loaded again with survivors, cargo and Midori, again swung out over the deck. The swimmers in the water bobbed up and down like corks. And now one head, arms flailing in helplessness, was going under, lashing at the waves.

Harry Connerly stirred from his apathy.

The struggling girl in the water, for it was a female, sprung the lock within his brain and chest. Quickly, he slung his hat off, vaulted to the rail and dove into the sea, slicing the water with a clean, true plunge. In a few powerful strokes, he had reached the girl. Before she could falter further, he had steered her toward the safety of the rope ladder.

Charley Adams watched. Something came alive within her again. Pride shone out of her. Harry had saved the life of another human being. Connerly passed the limp, straining figure up to Rigby. Rigby nodded his approval. The young scientist's face was flushed and exhausted but thoroughly happy.

The final survivors had reached the safety of the decks of the *Batavia Queen*. The lifeboat stroked into position to connect its blocks. The davits creaked.

"Make fast the lifeboat!" Hanson roared. "Bring in the boarding ladder!" Hanson was in a hurry. He had not liked the warning ominous sounds from Krakatoa. They had been somehow of a different-caliber noise. Something else was cooking in that old buzzard. The sky was leaden and dull, the smoke-ash permeating every inch of atmosphere.

The sampan, empty and forlorn, had begun to slip slowly beneath the surface of the sea, sliding out of sight within seconds. A gasp went up from the survivors flocked along the rails, watching the fate of their most recent home.

Laura was wrapping Peter in a heavy blanket, hugging him still, her face lit up with a beautiful new radiance. Hanson shook off the image. There was still Krakatoa to consider and the fate of the ship. They weren't out of the woods yet. They had not yet cleared troubled waters.

Krakatoa's final hour had come, obviously. Hanson somehow sensed it, knew it. The mighty peak was a pure-white phosphoresent furnace on the horizon. A thunderous explosion suddenly burst in the distance, a tremendous, world-shaking roar of sound. Smoke, flame and dazzling light illuminated the sky. The sound penetrated the boards of the ship, making tied-down objects of equipment rattle. The *Queen* shuddered, lifting from the sea. The survivors uttered a universal wail of terror, their eyes pinned to the sight of the mighty Krakatoa's self-destruction. The final paroxysms of the terrible volcano had no equal in their range of experience. Nor had it in Hanson's or his crew's.

The burning light was blinding, the sound overwhelming. More explosions cannonaded. Giant dark clouds, tinged with crimson, fusing and spreading, covered the mantle of the volcano. The cone disappeared in a flash of kaleidoscoping maelstrom.

Charley Adams, Giovanni Borghese, Connerly and Squid moved slowly on the forward deck, drawn to the rail as if mesmerized. Wonder and amazement made them watch despite their fear. Crushing waves of extraordinary sound reached across the water to touch them, deafen them. Krakatoa's demise filled the heart and mind and soul.

Laura Travis clutched Peter to her bosom, frightened again. Disintegrating Krakatoa must not take her child from her. The rock mountain was tearing from the sea itself, the heavens streaked with fiery colors. The dying volcano split, coughed and came apart, an orgy of sight and sound.

The children, the priests, the nuns and Chinese seamen cringed under the volume of destruction, visible before them. Leoncavallo, a small, ironbound sea chest clutched under his arm, paused to look, too. But fear had left him with the death of Toshi. He was only aware of the fact that among the cargo salvaged from the sampan had been this ancient box which bore the nailed-on iron letters that spelled out the name "Travis." He had been quick to seize it.

The crew, the people, his father, everybody was too caught up in the death of Krakatoa to disturb them now. Treasures could wait.

The sound was subsiding, the white-hot furnace of Krakatoa tumbling into the sea. The mighty roar diminished, changing into a low hideous rumble of noise. The waters rose in the distance. The ship lurched. The cataclysm ended.

Leoncavallo looked at his father, the diver Connerly and his woman, Laura Travis and her son, Rigby the scientist, Hanson the captain and Toshi's friends, Kiko, Midori and Sumi. He held out the small chest to Laura Travis. She blinked.

"There are your pearls."

Hanson's first concern was the ship. "Mr. Jacobs, batten hatches, stow sail, make secure for heavy seas." Then he stared at Leoncavallo Borghese and the prize he held forward.

Leoncavallo set the chest on the deck floor. His father knelt, trying to open it. The lid did not move. The box was locked. Rigby frowned ruefully. "Damn! What a waste." The others looked at him in surprise.

"Gentlemen!" Hanson's curt tone was a command. "You've found them." He looked at Peter Travis, at his mother's side, gazing on in awe. "Peter, would you take the chest to the salon so we can see what you've brought us?"

Reluctantly, the boy pulled away from his mother. He picked up the small sea chest and dutifully trooped forward with it. Hanson and the members of the expedition followed him. Hanson's friendly smile did not go away as he left last instructions for Kuan.

"Mr. Kuan. I think we should get our passengers from the sampan below decks and under shelter. Then rig for storm."

Before going below decks to the salon, Hanson paused only to cast one last look toward Krakatoa. A last gesture, as it were.

The bright splash of violent color still hung in the sky. Beneath it, where the mighty Krakatoa had stood on the sea, there was nothing.

The group in the salon waited from force of habit for Hanson to show up. Giovanni Borghese, with a small smile, had relieved Peter Travis of the small iron chest and placed it on a table close to the bar. He had casually tried the lid but found it unyielding. Charley Adams, Harry Connerly, Laura Travis, Douglas Rigby, Kiko, Midori, and Sumi and Leoncavallo stood about, helplessly.

Fuming, Connerly tried the lid, also. It didn't budge for him, either.

"Where's the key?" he asked Laura Travis.

Before she could answer, Peter spoke up shyly.

"I have it."

As their shock registered in a mixture of gasps and smiles, he stripped a chain from around his neck. A tiny key dangled from the chain. Connerly took it without hesitation. He bent to the lock, his eyes squinting, when Laura demurred.

"Mr. Connerly. Perhaps we should wait for Captain Hanson. He'll be here in a moment."

"He'll get his share, whether he's here or not," Connerly snapped.

Giovanni Borghese purred smoothly. "The pearls won't melt, Mr. Connerly. We have time."

Douglas Rigby smiled faintly. "Mr. Connerly has lived on the sea. He knows better."

Leoncavallo's sneer was almost ugly. "*What* does he know?"

Rigby changed the subject. "About the tidal wave . . ." he began matter-of-factly, still the scientist.

There was another, newer monumental explosion. The shock wave rocked the ship. They all struggled for balance, feeling the floor tilt, the furniture slide. There was a moment of general astonishment before the vessel righted itself once more. The explosion faded from hearing. Charley Adams giggled nervously.

Hanson put in an appearance, hurrying down the stairs into the salon. There were two small children in his arms. Chinese faces, dark hair, frightened eyes.

". . . the one Captain Hanson is preparing for," Rigby concluded calmly.

Leoncavallo streaked for the nearest porthole. Looking out, he gasped. "It's disappeared! Krakatoa's gone!"

"*Tsunami!*" There was stark horror in Midori as she uttered the word. Kiko and Sumi began to jabber excitedly, a frightened medley of Japanese words.

"Tidal wave!" Rigby explained for Giovanni Borghese's benefit. Leoncavallo's father was blank with wonder at the behavior of the diving girls.

Hanson set the children down. They scampered into a corner of the salon. A squad of crewmen, carrying hammers, canvas, lines and heavy screw eyes came thundering down the stairs. With a quick gesture, Hanson set them working on the lounge, preparing the salon for the expected disaster.

"Chris," Laura Travis cried. "I've just got him back . . ." She hugged Peter to her. He spread his hands to show her how sorry and helpless he was in the face of the elements.

"We'll be ready for it, Laura."

Now, the sodden, newly terrified survivors of the sampan came scurrying down into the salon. Charley Adams watched them with disbelief, reading futility and dread in all the strange foreign faces. Her normally strong personality had taken too much of a battering these last few days.

"After all this aren't we gonna make it, Harry?" Her tone

rose hysterically. Connerly hushed her with a wave of his arm. Her fright was contagious. A survivor whimpered. Hanson slammed a heavy book down on the table to achieve silence. And control.

"We have a chance if we get to deep water. Now please listen to me—"

Connerly halted at his opening of the metal chest.

"Deep water, hell! We're almost to Anjer."

"The wave will crush Anjer," Hanson said with icy authority. "We might ride it out at sea."

At the forward bulkhead, the crewmen were hammering away, setting large screw eyes into the paneling, stringing line on the wall to secure the passengers. A general rig to combat the expected onslaught of millions of gallons of water unleashed in a tidal wave of crushing force.

"At sea?" Giovanni Borghese asked dubiously.

Connerly exploded. "Not me. Put us ashore."

"Mr. Connerly," Hanson was angry now. "You are a man of the sea. You know I can't possibly get in and get out of Anjer fast enough to save the ship."

The stairway was flooded with sailors carrying armloads of mattresses, blankets and pillows. For a moment the chest of pearls stood forgotten. Peter Travis whispered to his mother. "What's happening?"

She knelt to him, an island of calm amid the turmoil.

"When a great amount of land is displaced on a seacoast, Peter," she murmured warmly, comfortingly, "a tremendous wave of water rushes in to take its place. It is called a tidal wave." She put her arm around him as if not to infect him with her own anxiety.

Borghese looked to Hanson for an answer. "What about the lifeboat, Captain Hanson?"

Hanson was annoyed. "Why are you asking me about lifeboats at a time like this?"

"Give it to us," Connerly ordered.

Hanson stared at him.

"Are you serious?"

"Sure!" Connerly's face was set. "There's no other way to make land. I'm not gonna ride out a tidal wave in *this* bucket."

Hanson's reaction to that was nearly physical. He stepped for Connerly, his face furious. Borghese moved deftly between them. He pointed to his son, Leoncavallo.

"We too will go, Captain."

"And we, sir." Midori spoke for herself and her two friends.

Hanson studied their faces for a moment, fighting with himself. The anger in him would not go away. Tightly, barely controlling his fury, he said gratingly: "You will *die* in Anjer, do you realize that?"

There was only an instant's silence. Midori broke it quietly.

"Sir . . . please?" The native face, the dignity, the calm majesty of the girl did more than anything Connerly had said. Hanson could understand that an island woman might well wish to go back to the land if she had to die. Even a woman whose livelihood was diving. The death of Toshi still haunted him.

"Take it," Hanson said coldly.

"We thank you," Borghese said.

"It's no favor."

Connerly finally opened the chest with Peter's key. The light of hundreds of clustered pearls was reflected in the awed faces surrounding the open box. The treasure was real. Their imaginations had not lied to them. The promise that the *Adrianna* had held out to them all since the very beginning of the expedition had not been false. The Travis treasure in pearls would make millionaires of them all. For a long, breathtaking interval, no one could say very much.

"You have less than twenty minutes," Hanson snapped, breaking the spell of gold, "to reach Anjer, and find high ground."

Connerly immediately dug into the chest, shoveling out two handfuls of the pearls. These he placed in a small sack. Giovanni Borghese and Midori moved past him to take their shares. Charley Adams could only watch Harry Connerly, wondering if he had lost his senses. Hanson should know what he was talking about.

"Harry, if Mr. Hanson says the ship is safer—"

"Safe?" He dropped the sack of pearls inside his shirt, buttoning up rapidly. "Who else is ready?" He didn't bother answering her.

"We are," Borghese announced, brushing his hands.

"Yes, sir," Midori said, speaking for all again.

Giovanni held a gem-filled handkerchief in one hand. With the other he clasped Leoncavallo's shoulder, steering him toward the stairway. Hanson's hammering crew filled the salon with a racket of noise and activity.

"Father . . ." Leoncavallo held back.

Borghese offered the handkerchief to the young man. He shook his head.

"I'm not going," Leoncavallo said simply.

Before Borghese could evince his astonishment, Connerly

pushed past him. He stopped only because Charley Adams had not moved. She was standing by the sea chest, fearful, uncertain.

"C'mon, Charley," Connerly said gruffly.

She didn't move. Connerly growled, "Charley!" She didn't answer him. Suddenly, the face of the deep-sea diver crumpled, showing how he truly needed this woman to sustain him. The blond woman was his base of power and confidence in himself. "Charley!" he roared.

She turned at the plea in his cry. Terrified, she appealed to his better judgment.

"We won't make it, Harry."

"Sure we will, honey."

"Come with me, Leoncavallo." Borghese tried to take his son's arm again. The boy shook his head. There was no fear in him. Only a sense of his own worth motivated him.

"C'mon, Charley," Connerly was saying softly, smiling encouragement. "Have I ever steered you wrong?"

She wavered. Finally, she came, sure in her heart that they were going without a prayer of survival. But she was Harry Connerly's woman, and by her code, that meant she would follow him into hell if that was what he wanted.

Harry Connerly and Charley Adams disappeared up the stairway. Douglas Rigby ascended behind them, saying nothing, suggesting nothing.

Borghese looked at his son.

"Leoncavallo—" he began.

"I don't want to die with you, Father. I want us to live together."

The older man smiled. A long slow smile.

"Since you were a little fellow . . . a handsome, intelligent . . . stubborn little fellow, I have hoped that something would happen. A word, a gesture, that would bind us together for the rest of our lives. And now that we've found it—"

"Father, I'm still stubborn but I want to live as much as you do."

"Then we must go ashore."

"There won't be any shore. It will be under a hundred feet of water."

"Then the ship will go like a matchstick," Borghese said emphatically.

"A matchstick floats, Father," Leoncavallo said.

Giovanni Borghese sighed. A long sigh.

"We always argue." He shrugged in the old grand manner.

"But maybe it won't be as bad as Captain Hanson says. Either on the ship or at Anjer."

It was sheer Florentine bravado. But most necessary to both men.

"We'll be together soon," Leoncavallo agreed.

Their eyes touched. And then their arms swept around each other. Borghese held him for a tight, loving embrace. They broke apart.

"Good-bye, my son."

"Father," Leoncavallo said proudly, "I love you." He spoke the words in Italian. *"Ti amo."*

Giovanni Borghese lowered his head, turned away and hurried up the stairs. After a moment, Leoncavallo followed, walking slowly. The Oriental girls rushed past him, fear making them run. They flitted like birds before they disappeared.

Hanson had put an arm around Peter Travis' shoulder and another around Laura and piloted them toward the bulkhead. Cushions had been placed protectively against the salon wall. A veritable stack of comfort and safety. Cushions torn from the salon itself.

"Peter," Hanson said, "this will be very exciting for you. Laura, if you will sit next to him . . ."

With the aid of several crewmen, Hanson began to rope the boy and his mother to the bulkhead. Peter was very frightened by all the preparations but was covering it very well. Laura Travis was only frightened for the men in her life.

"You will be all right," Hanson murmured, patting the boy's face.

Laura nodded positively. "Will *you*, Chris?"

"I'm fine," he said.

He smiled at Peter and slapped the boy's shoulder in a hearty man-to-man gesture.

"We're all going to be fine."

All about them, the crewmen continued fortifying the salon. Hammer noises and the metallic bite of nails into wood sounding like the building of a mammoth coffin.

Hanson did not like the sound.

Douglas Rigby had stationed himself at the rail above the boarding ladder to make his farewells to all those who were quitting the ship. He shook hands with each of them silently, in a wordless well-wishing. The drab gray sky was threatening.

Connerly slung a leg over the rail and descended quickly. Borghese and Leoncavallo were close behind. At the last moment, the father handed the packet of pearls to his son and stepped over the rail, beginning to climb down. Startled, Leoncavallo tried to hand the pearls back but Borghese did not look at him, dropping into the waiting lifeboat. Charley Adams nervously mounted the rail, going down the ladder. Her tall shapely body swayed. Rigby assisted her. She smiled her thanks. Then she too entered the boat.

"Father?" Leoncavallo called out. There was no answer. The boy turned away.

The Japanese girls dropped their small packages to Connerly. Climbing the rail, they disappeared also. Rigby and Leoncavallo were alone at the head of the ladder. Two seamen were helping the shore party get under way.

Seamen busy with other matters were bustling about on deck. Working high in the rigging, preparing the aft and stern and midships for the coming tidal wave. Squid chanted a native song, his giant's body working powerfully. Dark clouds raced overhead.

The tiny lifeboat pushed out into the angry sea. Connerly and Borghese were at the oars, rowing quickly. Within seconds, the boat grew smaller, pointing toward Anjer and the unseen shore. Borghese looked back as he rowed, keeping Leoncavallo in view as long as possible. Charley Adams sat straight-backed in fear. The smile had been removed from her personality, perhaps forever. The girls, Kiko, Midori and Sumi, sat quietly in the stern, their Oriental faces mute.

Hanson stood at the hatch, watching the lifeboat recede into the darkening shadows. The waves were already tumultuous, lashing and rising. The skies seethed with portentous movement.

Jacobs, urging the two seamen who had assisted in the launching of the lifeboat to bring in the lines and make fast the davits, called down to Hanson from the bridge.

"Full ahead, Captain?"

Hanson waved a confirming hand without taking his eyes off the lifeboat, growing smaller and smaller before fading into the mist.

"Full ahead!" Jacobs bellowed, his hard shout filling the air, expressing the desire to get going, to get the hell out of harm's way.

Leoncavallo and Rigby left the rail. The lifeboat was gone. Hanson remained on the hatch staring out at the gathering darkness. A boatload of fools going where sensible angels would fear to tread.

Anjer.

It lay in the very path of the tidal wave.

But that was no concern of his now. His first consideration was the *Batavia Queen* and the race for deep water.

The Argus Point lighthouse outside of Anjer Harbor echoed with the metallic stutter of the telegraph. The caretaker of the tower, a stocky, stolid-faced Dutchman, raised a pair of binoculars and looked out to sea. The sight was grim. Huge breakers rolled in, their white caps scarcely visible in the dark gray overcast skies. Anjer Harbor, directly behind the lighthouse, was a massive agitation of tossing waves, rocking boats and frantically moving craft of every description. The smaller craft were making for anchorage as fast as their sails would carry them. The caretaker felt uneasy in his stomach. A bad one was coming all right; if he stirred himself to answer the telegraph, he was afraid of what he would find out. He wasn't deaf. Old Krakatoa had been making an infernal racket all day and then there had been that last whopping explosion . . .

He had never seen the sky looking so ugly before. Like the ending of the world. Clouds boiling, heavy masses of color streaking along, all gathering for a big blow.

Or something like a tidal wave.

Frightened, the caretaker put the glasses down and reached for the telegraph key.

The news was coming in now . . .

It wasn't good. Not good at all.

The pistons in the engine room of the *Batavia Queen* were laboring mightily, their noise filling the steaming room. The boilers were going full blast. The entire ship was responding to the emergency. Hanson's orders were swiftly, efficiently, obeyed.

Butterfly III had been lashed securely in the hold, the fantail hatch door clanged shut. The steel plate of the boat deck hatch slid tightly closed. The deck awnings were rolled in. Ropes were made secure across the canvas cover of the aft hatch. The engine room skylight doors were slammed shut. All the loose objects in Hanson's cabin were stored in chests and trunks and closets by Kuan and a seaman. Whatever wasn't nailed down, Hanson was having fastened or put away where it couldn't bang loose.

Hanson's most important instruction was to First Officer Jacobs.

"Tell them we'll give a general warning with the ship's whistle just before we take the wave."

The huge propellor screw was churning viciously, fighting the changing ferocity of the ocean. Hanson ordered a tight turn of the ship, leaving a foaming wake at the stern. The steamer plowed firmly through the sea.

Hanson asked Leoncavallo Borghese and Douglas Rigby to assist belowdecks, helping with the cargo of passengers and the women. When he entered the wheelhouse, the sky had truly transformed into a darkened curtain of roiling clouds and mists. He crossed to the chart table and placed a forefinger on the map.

"Argus Point lighthouse. Anjer . . . and . . . us. What does it show?"

"Ten fathoms," Jacobs said flatly.

"Not enough. Any more muscle left in those engines?"

"We can find out."

They were rigged for the heavy sea now. Whatever was coming, they'd be ready for it. As ready as possible.

Seamen marched into the wheelhouse, going around locking all the windows. A great gale was coming up off the starboard bow, fanning the decks, making the ship lurch. Hanson waited.

He had done many things as a sailor in his life.

But this was his very first tidal wave.

And the *Batavia Queen*'s.

He wished the both of them luck.

At Anjer, the lifeboat had finally reached the questionable safety of shore. Through a hail of ash and smoke, the occupants scrambled onto dry land. Behind them, the mountainous seas had begun to rise, to slap the coast awesomely, to make the ground shudder. Connerly, Charley Adams, Borghese and the girl divers, all rushed for the interior. The jungle-like countryside that held the higher ground. Where there were high places, with trees.

The tidal wave was but minutes behind them. Gathering up the tremendous forces of water, wind and storm to hurl itself against the defenseless shore.

Before it reached the land itself, the tidal wave claimed its first victim. The Argus Point lighthouse. The caretaker, terrified at the tremendous height of the wall of water rushing in from the ocean, backed away until the far wall stopped him. He could not retreat farther. The world had ended for him as the wave hit.

The tower crumbled, paper-like, swallowed up in the massive juggernaut of water pounding toward the town of Anjer. Toward the horrified community of men and women, Oriental and Occidental alike, rushing desperately into the hills to escape. Ancient carts and creaking wagons lumbered over the knolls and ridges, fighting for the safety of higher earth. There wasn't land high enough, really. Hanson had unfortunately been accurate in his estimate of the power and force of the wave.

Giovanni Borghese found a tall, grotesquely gnarled tree. The tree seemed ageless. Formidable. Borghese helped Kiko, Midori and Sumi to climb it. They situated themselves in its ancient limbs, waiting. The thunderous cataract of sound behind them, the building roar of the wave, shut out every other sound in the universe. Every other hope. The girls whimpered. Borghese tried to see, to smile through the ordeal.

Connerly and Charley Adams had gained an open-fronted warehouse on the outskirts of Anjer. All around them, the sheds and frame buildings vibrated and trembled, lashed by heavy tides and winds. Connerly shoved Charley under the shelter of a flimsy-roofed godown. He planted his body across hers protectively.

A huge wave loomed monstrously, crashing in from the now filling streets of the town. Destroying everything in its path, the raging tide swept on toward Connerly and Charley Adams.

Charley saw it coming, her eyes opened in disbelief, her lips trembled. Then she buried her golden face in Connerly's shoulder. Harry Connerly held her trembling body, taking one last despairing look himself. Then he, too, looked away.

The giant wave rolled over them.

Borghese and the girls gaped at the oncoming water and the great destruction it brought with it. Anjer was vanishing before their eyes. The girls clung to one another, crying out in their native tongue. Borghese reacted more in surprise than fear. Wonderment was on his face, very nearly the appreciation of a showman for a spectacular theatrical production. One whose like he had never seen before. Whose like he would not see again.

And then the incredible mass of water engulfed him, the girls and their tree.

The town of Anjer vanished beneath the waves.

Swirling, churning, boiling, completely obliterated from the face of the earth.

The humanity straining for the higher ground could not outrun the lightning-bolt rapidity of the great waters rushing behind them.

The end had come for Anjer and all its inhabitants.

The scream of the steam whistle blasted the gloom.

The *Batavia Queen* rocked in the very teeth of the phenomenon. The tremendously high waves lifted the steamer like a cork. Hanson, at the helm, fought it with all his power and knowledge. He had locked the wheel, securing it in position. Jacobs, Kuan and Jan had found sitting positions, bracing their backs to the forward bulkhead. Hanson jumped to the telegraph, jamming it to *Full Ahead*.

"If we're caught broadside," he muttered. He didn't finish the statement. The threat in it hung like a pall over the wheelhouse. Beyond the locked windows, the ocean buffeted, stormed, lashed at the ship. The undulating wave, over a hundred feet high, thundered forward.

Hanson held on to his nerves, joining the men on the floor. He closed his eyes.

There was nothing to do now but pray.

Outside, the holocaust howled like all the devils in hell. The *Batavia Queen* shuddered from prow to stern.

In the salon, the children were all strapped in place. Laura Travis, Peter, the nuns and the priests were secured also. One of the nuns, a gentle-faced woman, held a squirming, frightened child in her arms. The nun began to sing, in a soft, warm voice. The howl of the weather beyond the salon windows was a counterpoint of terror and disaster.

"Sister, Sister, have you heard . . . I know a word that's a magic word . . ."

Soon, others began to pick up the familiar melody. Laura and Peter clung to one another, staring. Then they too began to sing. Suddenly, the urgent shrill of the steam whistle shattered through the singing voices and the noises of the sea. There was a petrified silence and the gradually building sound of the tidal wave came to them. Again, the shaky-voiced, frail choir started up. Another whistle blast came but the singing did not stop this time.

In the forward hold, Hanson's crew took their defensive positions among the stored cargo. This was it. The captain's notice that the tidal wave was in sight and on the way. Grimly, the seamen braced themselves. The hollow pounding of the ship engines thundered faintly against the louder sound of the wind.

The sea was roaring like a locomotive. The eye-bulging view from the wheelhouse window was staggering. The mountainous wave was rushing forward, awesome in size and elemental grandeur. Hanson released the steam whistle and sawed desperately at the wheel. The boat was not in line to meet the wave head-on.

"Jacobs, full ahead, all full!"

The first officer scrambled to his feet, grabbed the telegraph, completing the signal to the engine room. Hanson hauled on the steam whistle cord once more.

The ship bobbed, turned slowly, came sluggishly about, defiantly presenting her prow to the oncoming wave. Now the ship headed directly into the mountainous pile of water, which towered sixty feet above her decks. The water hit. A plunging, gigantic cataract of violence. The *Batavia Queen* was thrown back, shuddering, shaking angrily as if it would split in half. The bowsprit crumpled, the rigging disintegrated, the twin masts buckled. The sea filled the decks, roaring incredibly like some engine of destruction. The gigantic wave rolled forward.

Water crashed through the windows of the salon and the engine room, gushing into the interiors, flooding the confines. Hanson, in the wheelhouse, was flung backward, smashed to the floor. An enormous humming, vibrating sound filled his brain.

The salon tilted sharply, torrents cascading down the stairway, drowning the space. Rigby, Leoncavallo and two of the seamen not safely lashed, toppled like tenpins, hurled sprawling with the racing tide. A Chinese child cried out in terror. Peter Travis buried his face in his mother's lap. Laura closed her eyes.

Bales, crates, cartons and boxed cargo in the packed hold tore loose, spilling down on the crewmen huddled in their vicinity. The water rushed on, hurtling forward, streaming through the very entrances it had made, continuing on toward some nameless destination. Seamen shouted, crying out in confusion and pain. There were injured now; among these,

Engine Room Chief Driscoll and the winch operator, Sullivan.

The holocaust whirled on. Maddening, fearsome.

Squid strained to hold two enormous bales apart as crewmen hauled Driscoll and Sullivan to safety. The waters receded, pushing on.

There was a long moment of pounding, thunderous violence in which the universe reeled under one enormous blow. And then came the miraculous shifting of weight, space and time.

Rolling in the aftermath of the fantastic deluge, the *Batavia Queen* righted herself. With an agonizing slowness, a mighty shudder. A unified groan and wrench of movement. A heavy list to port and the ship trembled erectly. Firmly, unsinkably. The drenched bows shook themselves the way a dog does after an unwanted dousing. The ship heeled but held steady.

Hanson struggled to his feet, gaining the helm once more. His face was a mask; the wheelhouse rippled with watery illusiveness. At first apprehension filled him, then a dawning, hard-to-believe relief. He helped the stunned, tousled Jacobs to his feet. He almost smiled. Jan and Kuan had righted themselves off the dripping, glass-strewn deck. Kuan was amazed, his bland face sputtering.

"We made it," he said, shocked.

Hanson nodded. His ship had performed the impossible. It had ridden out a tidal wave. Pride and happiness sung in his veins.

"Yes," he said slowly.

His officers stared at him.

"Get the broken rigging cut right away. We've a heavy cargo shift and taken plenty of water. But she's holding, bless her. Fix it. I'll be below." There was a trace of a wry smile in his words. Kuan grinned.

"Go ahead," Jacobs muttered. "I'll pick up the pieces."

Hanson exited quickly. Jacobs looked at Jan and Kuan as they went to the wheel to test its response.

"Fix it!" Jacobs repeated wonderingly.

There was never any telling about Captain Chris Hanson.

The worst weather in the world would never stop him from being a rules and regulations skipper.

A damned great seaman.

The salon room was devastated.

Forty pairs of eyes swept over Hanson as he descended the battered stairs. Rigby and Leoncavallo were tending to the still-frightened, bewildered sampan survivors. The salon was a shambles. Water on the floor, inches deep, blankets, pillows and cushions all crushed and strewn about like so many scattered bits of wreckage. The broken windows, broken furniture and damaged bar would never be the same again. It had a curious effect on Hanson. He paused for a moment to take in the wreckage of the salon that had known so many fine parties and sailing celebrations on the *Batavia Queen*.

It was a sad sight, but he brightened when he saw Laura Travis' lovely face. And Peter's little-boy gladness to see him.

Peter jumped off his mother's lap, sloshing across the floor to meet him. Hanson hugged the boy, still staring at his mother. She was flooded with relief and pride and joy, too. Proud of her captain and their survival.

Before Hanson could touch her, kiss her, a tiny sobbing sound spoiled their moment. Hanson turned, still holding on to Peter Travis.

A tiny Chinese girl, left alone on the couch in one corner of the big room, was starting to cry. Tension, excitement and terror had been too much for her. Big tears rolled down her oval cheeks.

Leoncavallo crossed the floor swiftly to her. He smiled a sad smile. Scooping her young body off the floor, he cuddled the little Oriental child in his arms.

Giovanni Borghese's handsome son began to sing. A faint, soft melody that all in the salon were now familiar with.

"Sister, Sister, have you heard . . . If I should wish I could be a bird . . ." His voice was melodious and strong. A man's voice comforting a child.

Douglas Rigby, kneeling at the side of one of the nuns, untying a knotted rope, turned to watch. The nun did, too.

"If I should wish I could fly through the blue . . . If I should wish and say Kee kana lu . . ."

The child stopped crying, staring yearningly at him.

"Kee kana lu-oo . . . Kee kana lu . . ." Leoncavallo's voice was filled with sadness. Hanson looked down at Peter. The boy was rapt in the loveliness of the song.

"Kee kana lu-oo . . . kee kana lu . . ."

Leoncavallo started up the angled stairway, cradling the child in his arms. His voice had fallen almost to a crooning lullaby of a whisper. The child was dry-eyed now.

Douglas Rigby smiled after him.

Hanson and Laura and Peter walked toward the stairway

too, hands clasped. The ship was turning now, easing slightly in her course. Hanson looked at Laura. Their eyes talked to each other.

The almost broken *Batavia Queen* limped toward the far horizon. A strange hue colored the sky. The dust, the ash, the vapor that was Krakatoa, still hovered over the sea, in the wake of the awesome tidal wave that had come and was now gone.

The monster was finally sleeping eternally.

For Hanson, it was the beginning of a new life for himself. And Laura. And Peter.

What the sea took, it sometimes gave back.

Other Recent SIGNET Mysteries

☐ **ELLERY QUEEN'S ALL-STAR LINE-UP by Ellery Queen.** Suspense of every variety by such mystery pros as John Creasey, Charlotte Armstrong, Georges Simenon, Stanley Ellin, and even a mystery "discovery" by William Shakespeare. (#T3698—75¢)

☐ **THE EVER-LOVING BLUES by Carter Brown.** Danny Boyd accepts a movie mogul's bid to track down a wandering, wanton star and winds up playing footsy with a couple of thugs on a 15th century Spanish galleon in Florida. (#D3722—50¢)

☐ **THE FLAGELLATOR by Carter Brown.** Fleur Falaise, superstar, was worth millions dead. When her "suicide" failed, she was locked in her room with a militant nurse and a secretary who would put Lolita to shame. Then the Flagellator arrived—and fast on his heels, Rick Holman, private eye. (#D3776—50¢)

☐ **DEATH TO MY BELOVED by Richard Neely.** A psychotic killer lashes vengeance from San Francisco to New York leaving a scarlet trail of murder, blackmail and sex, and a publisher's empire falls in an explosion of scandal. (#P3742—60¢)

☐ **TOPSY AND EVIL by George Baxt.** A way-out, free-swinging mystery about Satan Stagge, a hip Negro detective, whose job it is to find out why Pharoah Love has disappeared when tycoon Guru Raskalnikov is bludgeoned to death with the classic blunt instrument. (#P3767—60¢)

☐ **HEIST ME HIGHER by Bill S. Ballinger.** A real sock-it-to-'em mystery about Private Eye Bryce Patch and his two cases—one to find the killer of an old friend and the other commissioned in the queen sized bed of an ex-show girl looking for her ex-husband. (#P3799—60¢)

THE NEW AMERICAN LIBRARY, INC., P.O. Box 2310, Grand Central Station, New York, New York 10017

Please send me the SIGNET BOOKS I have checked above. I am enclosing $_____(check or money order—no currency or C.O.D.'s). Please include the list price plus 10¢ a copy to cover mailing costs. (New York City residents add 5% Sales Tax. Other New York State residents add 2% plus any local sales or use taxes.)

Name_____

Address_____

City_____ State_____ Zip Code_____

Allow at least 3 weeks for delivery

Other Recent SIGNET Mysteries

☐ **THE SOURCE OF FEAR by Bill S. Ballinger.** Two men and a beautiful woman cross paths on a blood-chilling excursion to a lost city of sin and its legendary treasure. (#P3655—60¢)

☐ **A MURDER OF QUALITY by John Le Carré.** England's oldest and finest public school plays host to murder, and George Smiley exercises his quit and penetrating ability to solve the crime. By the author of **The Spy Who Came in from the Cold.** (#T3667—75¢)

☐ **A CALL FOR THE DEAD by John Le Carré.** George Smiley plays out the deadly game of international espionage in England and East Germany, as he investigates the case of a colleague's suicide. (#T3668—75¢)

☐ **THE DEEP COLD GREEN by Carter Brown.** Lt. Al Wheeler becomes number one target for a pack of card-carrying corpse makers, when he meets a sexy doll who calls herself Tracy Tenison. (#D3623—50¢)

☐ **GOD SAVE THE MARK by Donald E. Westlake.** Winner of the Mystery Writers of America "Edgar" for the best novel of the year, this zany romp was called by **The New York Times Book Review** critic, "a delightful comedy of character, and a brief encyclopedia on the art of the con, long and short." Coming as a Warner Bros.-Seven Arts movie. (#T3625—75¢)

☐ **HAWAII FIVE-O by Michael Avallone.** Based on the CBS television series, this fast-paced adventure novel conveys the turbulent atmosphere of the fiftieth state—exotic, beautiful, and the deadliest "beat" in the world for the men of the special police force assigned to keep order. (#P3622—60¢)

THE NEW AMERICAN LIBRARY, INC., P.O. Box 2310, Grand Central Station, New York, New York 10017

Please send me the SIGNET BOOKS I have checked above. I am enclosing $_____(check or money order—no currency or C.O.D.'s). Please include the list price plus 10¢ a copy to cover mailing costs. (New York City residents add 5% Sales Tax. Other New York State residents add 2% plus any local sales or use taxes.)

Name_____

Address_____

City_____State_____Zip Code_____

Allow at least 3 weeks for delivery